TAV

CELEBRITY
JUMPING EXERCISES

COMPILED BY
CAROLINE ORME

D&C
David and Charles

A DAVID & CHARLES BOOK
Copyright © David & Charles Limited 2006, 2009

David & Charles is an F+W Media Inc. company
4700 East Galbraith Road
Cincinnati, OH 45236

First published in the UK and USA in 2006

First UK paperback edition 2009

Text copyright © Caroline Orme, 2006, 2009
Photography copyright © Kit Houghton 2006, 2009 except photographs listed on page
135

ISBN-13: 978-0-7153-2253-6 hardback
ISBN-10: 0-7153-2253-2 hardback

ISBN-13: 978-0-7153-3298-6 paperback
ISBN-10: 0-7153-3298-8 paperback

A catalogue record for this book is available from the British Library.

Printed in China by SNP Leefung
for David & Charles
Brunel House   Newton Abbot   Devon

Commissioning Editor: Jane Trollope
Desk Editor: Jessica Deacon
Art Editor: Sue Cleave
Designer: Charly Bailey
Production Controller: Beverley Richardson

Visit our website at www.davidandcharles.co.uk

David & Charles books are available from all good bookshops; alternatively you can
contact our Orderline on 0870 9908222 or write to us at FREEPOST
EX2 110, D&C Direct, Newton Abbot, TQ12 4ZZ (no stamp required UK only);
US customers call 800-289-0963 and Canadian customers call 800-840-5220.

Contents

Foreword

Caroline Orme's compilation *Celebrity Jumping Exercises* is an interesting collection of exercises from a wide range of celebrities covering at least three generations. As such the exercises are many and varied, and give readers a small but significant insight into the thoughts and principles behind the jump training of the personalities involved.

To get the most out of this book readers must remember that there are in this life and especially with horses, many ways to skin a rabbit. Therefore as with all instruction you must pick the exercises you find work best for your horse, not necessarily the ones from the celebrity you admire the most!

You should also pick out the underlying themes that are common to most of the personalities. In particular remember that how you perform the exercise is more important than the exercise you pick. In this respect the quality of the gait in walk, trot and canter is of the utmost importance, as is the position of the rider in the 'middle' of the horse at all times, in the 'balanced seat'. Don't forget that whatever the gait, the approach should always be regular, smooth and even.

Another recurring theme is that the suppleness, rideability and adjustability of the horse is often more important than the ability. You will discover that you don't have to jump big fences to make a lot of these exercises difficult.

Confidence is another key and in this respect it is always easy to get carried away with your success. The secret to using these exercises successfully is always to stop while the horse is enjoying itself and never to go on until the fences become so difficult that the horse fails.

In short therefore, to get the most out of this book, cherry pick the exercises to suit you and your horse, always with one eye on your position and the quality of your horse's gait. That way these pages can only help you with your aims and ambitions as you share some of the secrets of these celebrities.

You will be able to keep this book as a reference for many years to come. Good luck with your horse and enjoy your jumping.

Captain Mark Phillips
January 2006

Guide to the Exercises

The following table will help you select a suitable exercise to work on if you are focusing on a particular issue. **Every exercise improves rhythm and balance.**

Type of work	Page number
Basic Principles	All Training Philosophies, 22
Warming up	26, 27, 94, 106
Improving straightness	10, 12, 30, 42, 46, 48, 50, 52, 56, 58, 62, 84, 98, 106, 108, 114, 116
Transitions	30, 94, 98, 128, 130
Enhancing the quality of the canter	
Impulsion	10, 14, 16, 28, 34, 48, 50, 52, 76, 78, 108, 118, 124, 126, 130
Shortening and lengthening	36, 66, 68, 84, 106, 125, 130
Related distances	12, 14, 28, 66, 68, 84, 100, 106, 108, 118, 120, 126, 128, 130
Turning	
In general	26, 27, 74, 76
Planning turns before and after fences	34, 68, 78, 80, 108, 116, 120, 124, 125, 130
Turning between fences	12, 14, 16, 28, 68, 80, 86, 88, 100, 108, 118, 120, 128, 130
Making good use of the arena	34, 130
Developing the jump	
Using grids	10, 12, 28, 30, 46, 48, 50, 52, 108, 114
Lunging	38
Solving specific jumping problems	36, 52, 98
Course work	42, 120, 125, 130
Improving accuracy	12, 16, 42, 58, 62, 80, 88, 90, 114, 116, 118, 120
Building instinctive reactions	12, 28, 34, 56, 120
Practising mock cross country fences	
Angles	12, 58, 80, 88, 116, 120
Corners	42, 90, 118
Bounces	10, 28, 48
Arrowheads and narrow fences	16, 42, 62, 114, 116, 120
Ditch, trakehner, coffin	56, 120

Key to the fences

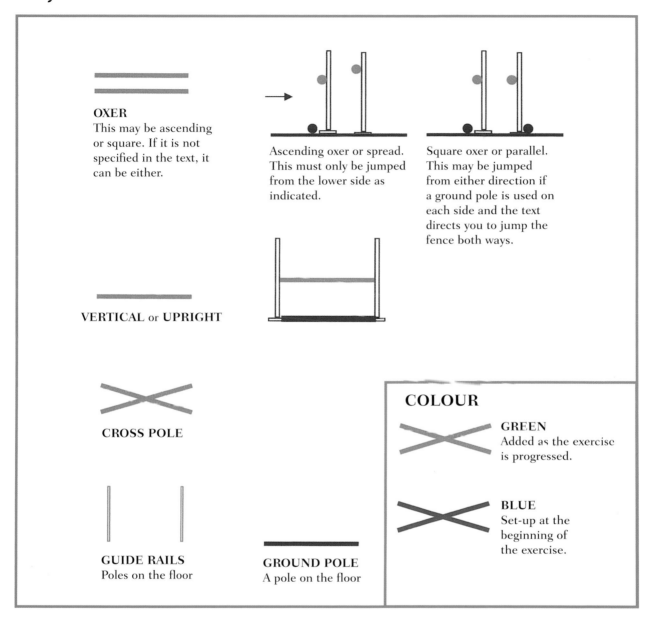

OXER
This may be ascending or square. If it is not specified in the text, it can be either.

Ascending oxer or spread. This must only be jumped from the lower side as indicated.

Square oxer or parallel. This may be jumped from either direction if a ground pole is used on each side and the text directs you to jump the fence both ways.

VERTICAL or **UPRIGHT**

CROSS POLE

GUIDE RAILS
Poles on the floor

GROUND POLE
A pole on the floor

COLOUR

GREEN
Added as the exercise is progressed.

BLUE
Set-up at the beginning of the exercise.

Distances

The distances between fences are given in metres, feet and paces. Everyone who show jumps must learn to walk a regular 3ft 'pace'. Although courses are measured metrically, riders pace the distances in feet, not metres. Measure a distance of 21 feet and regularly walk it so that you can set up fences and walk courses accurately. A pace is the same as a yard.

Pat Burgess

Yogi Breisner FBHS

Favourite achievements

★When horses I had worked with won the Champion Hurdle and Gold Cup at Cheltenham, it gave me a tremendous thrill of satisfaction. It was exciting to be part of the team involved with two horses winning such big races, and the whole atmosphere of Cheltenham made it a special occasion.

★It has given me a lot of satisfaction to be part of the success of the British event team over the last five years. It is especially rewarding to see the happiness that success gives to everyone when they are representing their country.

ADVICE TO NEWCOMERS

■ Seek help from someone who can give you a good, solid, basic education and a line to follow through your career. ENJOY IT.

(from left) Leslie Law, Zara Phillips, Jeanette Brakewell, William Fox-Pitt and Yogi Breisner receiving team gold at the Blenheim European championships.

Yogi began coaching the British senior team in 2000. Since then, they have brought home two Olympic team silver medals, an individual Olympic gold and an individual Olympic bronze. Under his guidance, the team has maintained their dominance of the European championships and won team bronze and individual silver at the World Equestrian Games in Jerez. Yogi's own competitive career included disciplines as diverse as dressage and point-to-pointing, and he represented Sweden as a member of its three-day-event team for over ten years. His rise to success as a trainer began in 1978 at Lars Sederholm's Waterstock House Training Centre, and in 1996 he was trainer for the Spanish event team at the Atlanta Olympics. Yogi has been a Fellow of the British Horse Society since 1992.

More… www.britisheventing.com (accredited trainers list)

TRAINING PHILOSOPHY

■ I work towards installing confidence and ensuring that horse and rider are enjoying their work. Installing confidence is a very individual situation depending on each of their strengths and weaknesses. Enjoying the work that is being done makes it easier for horses and riders to learn.

■ Leading up to a competition I work on getting riders to believe in themselves and their horses, and help with polishing up the final details. During a competition I stay in the background and provide help and support when needed.

Introduction to the exercises

Making use of specific exercises in your training will help the development of both horse and rider, and often makes life easier for the coach. While some exercises can be more beneficial than others, and certain exercises will work on specific areas, it is worth remembering that it is often not what you do, but how you do it that is important.

In the setting up of any exercise, there needs to be a clear objective of the aim, and it is often the simple exercises that work best. Each exercise should be progressive, with a start, middle and end. The first step of any exercise must be that the rider understands what to do, how to do it and why they are doing it. Some exercises might include the warm-up, while others require a separate warm-up. Whatever the exercise, a horse/rider/trainer must never deviate from the basics that are required for a horse to work and develop his best way of going. In jumping as in flatwork, these basics are: balanced rhythm, forward riding (the horse going forwards), pace, straightness and rider position. Throughout the execution of any exercise, rider and trainer need to check continuously that these basics are followed.

It often helps to use a specific exercise on consecutive days, as the horse and rider learn about it on the first day and can then use that knowledge to maximum effect on the second day. Continuing with the same exercise on the third day is not always beneficial, because once they are too familiar with it, complacency often sets in and they do not achieve the most from the experience. Whatever the exercise, it is worth remembering that all training must be fun and enjoyable, and that horse and rider learn best in a relaxed environment.

Line of five bounces

Uses

- To practise a cross-country fence and help maintain the horse's natural bascule
- To improve agility, reactions, straightness, rider's jumping technique and rider and horse confidence

Unsuitable for

- Very young and green horses
- Riders who have yet to develop a secure balance over single fences

This exercise gets horses used to bouncing, which is necessary for any event horse as this type of fence appears regularly on cross-country courses. It improves the horse's agility and reactions, and encourages him to leave the fence in the middle of the jump – that is, to make the highest part of his jump (bascule) over the middle of the fence (when viewed from the side). It teaches the rider to ride the horse on a level active stride on the approach, and is a very good exercise for working on a rider's position over a fence and making them aware of being in the middle and not ahead of the movement.

SETTING UP

- Place the poles off the track on the long side to allow maximum space to turn before and after the grids (diagram A).
- This exercise, and all its progressions, can be approached from both directions, making it easy to work evenly on both reins.

GETTING STARTED

1 Warm up over a single pole, and then add the rest of the poles one at a time (see diagram A).

2 To start the exercise, leave the poles on the floor and allow the horse to trot back and forth over them. As this distance is not always correct for a true trot stride, it encourages the horse to adjust his stride and be aware of objects in his way.

3 Let the horse canter over the poles on the floor. Either shorten the distance for cantering (2.7–3m/9–10ft, 3–3⅓ paces) to help the horse maintain a rhythm, or leave it as it is, in which case the rider will have to ride the horse slightly more forwards and encourage him to open and stretch his stride.

4 This exercise is best done by going up and down the line of fences rather than by staying on the same rein for any length of time.

PROGRESSING

5 When the work over the poles is finished, start with one cross pole and gradually build up until all five are at a suitable height for the experience of the horse (diagram B). Using cross poles rather than straight poles encourages the horse to jump the fence in the middle and to use himself better.

6 Once the horse is jumping through the line of five bounces in a confident manner, one can take out fences two and four (diagram C). The third (middle) fence should be significantly higher than either of the cross poles. The first cross pole helps to set up the horse for the bigger fence. Then the stride to that upright is generous enough to encourage the rider and the horse to go forwards, so that the horse takes one healthy stride without putting in an extra one.

7 If the distances are not adjusted, often the horse is encouraged to be slightly early in his take-off to the bigger fence. This either catches him out the first time (so he hits it), or immediately brings him up in the air and makes him try. The last cross pole encourages the horse to rebalance himself after the major effort of the middle fence.

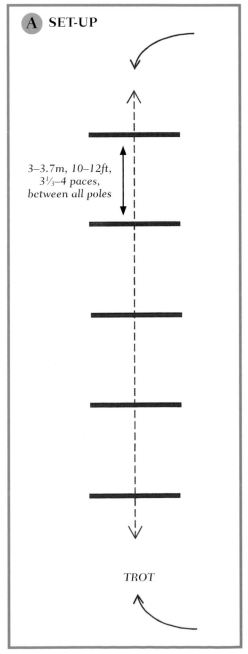

A SET-UP

3–3.7m, 10–12ft, 3⅓–4 paces, between all poles

TROT

Warm up over a single pole, in trot and canter. Then add the rest of the poles one at a time.

How to ride it

■ **The rider must maintain their balance** in the middle of the horse and not get ahead of the movement.

Fixing common faults

Panicking: If the horse is panicky through the five bounces and therefore goes faster and faster, jumping further beyond each fence, he will end up landing closer and closer to the next bounce. This encourages bad technique. Go back several steps to regain his trust. Try to anticipate situations your horse may find stressful and progress more slowly through them to avoid problems.

Putting in extra strides (diagram C): Are you approaching the first cross pole with enough impulsion (energy) and a balanced and rhythmic canter? An extra stride after the central fence is really the same problem – the horse has lost impulsion or is not taking big enough strides. Go large and work on shortening and lengthening to help energize the canter before returning to the exercise.

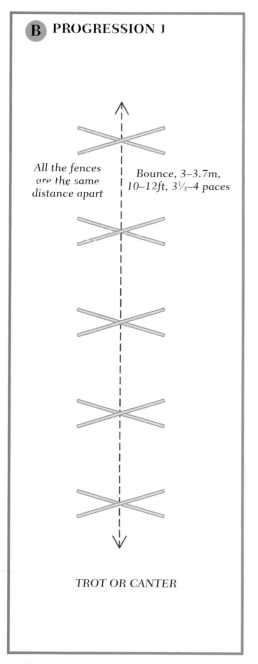

B PROGRESSION 1

All the fences are the same distance apart

Bounce, 3–3.7m, 10–12ft, 3⅓–4 paces

TROT OR CANTER

Build the grid slowly, one fence at a time.

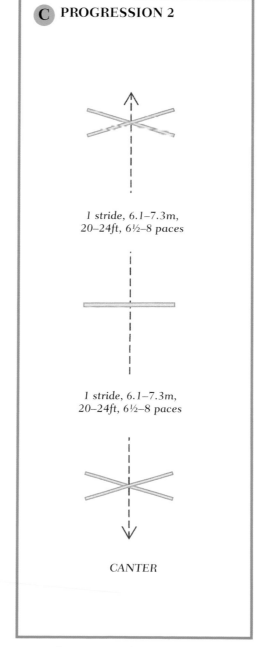

C PROGRESSION 2

1 stride, 6.1–7.3m, 20–24ft, 6½–8 paces

1 stride, 6.1–7.3m, 20–24ft, 6½–8 paces

CANTER

Remove fences two and four. Leave the distance as it is.

Distances shown are approximate and will depend on the horse.

Line of five or seven fences

Uses

- To practise a cross-country fence
- To develop fitness and improve the quality of the jump, canter and speed of reactions
- To get the horse used to lines of several jumps

Unsuitable for

- A small working area
- Horses below Novice eventing level
- Young inexperienced horses and riders who are not balanced enough to execute the turns

This exercise gives the rider the opportunity to practise difficult doglegs and fences at an angle. It helps the horse to maintain the same pace throughout a line of fences, which improves his rhythm and encourages him to slow down over each fence, so that he makes the jump more deliberate. It is important to execute both parts of this exercise as the second part ensures that the horse still goes straight.

Bear in mind that this is a testing exercise for horses and riders even if they are already used to jumping angles. It includes many changes of bend that can be unbalancing for inexperienced horses.

SETTING UP

- Build a line of five or seven fences in the centre of the working area with a ground line on each side of each one. The number of fences used depends on the experience of horse and rider and the space available.
- Do not use cross poles for this exercise.
- The fences should be equally spaced, each one canter stride apart.

GETTING STARTED

1 While the rider warms up the horse on the flat, they can do serpentine lines in and out of the fences of the exercise (see diagram A).

2 With the fences at a suitable height, start jumping individual fences at an angle. However far the angling is progressed, complete the exercise by riding straight through the line of fences.

PROGRESSING

3 Jump fences one, four and seven (or fences one and five if only five fences are used), see route 1, diagram B.

4 Then jump fences one, three, five and seven on a serpentine line (route 2, diagram B). If five fences are used, jump one, three and five.

5 For the second part of the exercise, jump back and forth over all the fences in a straight line (route 3, diagram B). Vary the size of the fences, so you jump a bigger fence, followed by a smaller fence, then a bigger one and a smaller one. The bigger fences will encourage the horse to make an effort while the smaller ones will give him a breather and lift his confidence, whereupon he then has to make an effort again, and so on.

6 This exercise will require a lot of jumping from the horse during the session, which will also help his fitness. Be aware of not overdoing it. Horse and rider could finish off by jumping a single fence, such as a spread, since they have just been working over upright fences.

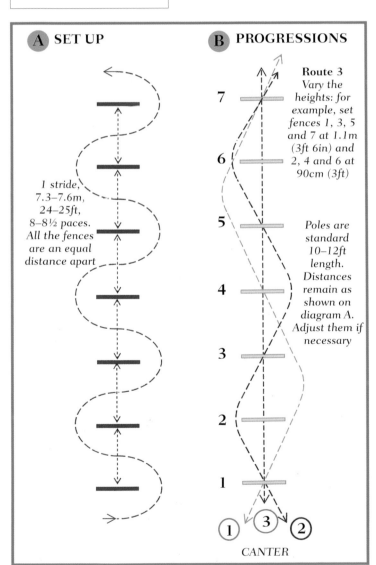

A SET UP

1 stride, 7.3–7.6m, 24–25ft, 8–8½ paces. All the fences are an equal distance apart

B PROGRESSIONS

7

6

5

4

3

2

1

Route 3
Vary the heights: for example, set fences 1, 3, 5 and 7 at 1.1m (3ft 6in) and 2, 4 and 6 at 90cm (3ft)

Poles are standard 10–12ft length. Distances remain as shown on diagram A. Adjust them if necessary

① ③ ②

CANTER

Place five or seven upright fences in a straight line with a ground line on each side of each fence.

Follow the above routes in the order shown.

Distances

- Adjust the distances depending on the horse.
- These distances are for fences about 1.1m (3ft 6in) high. For smaller fences, shorten them by 30cm (1ft) or so.

How to ride it

- **Make sure the horse is not pulled around** when ridden through the doglegs but follows a nice smooth line where the rider is more guiding than steering the horse through the turn.
- **Notice the number of strides between jumps** (routes 1 and 2) and keep them even and rhythmic.
- **Canter lead** (routes 1 and 2) You can approach the first fence with the correct lead to get to the next, but should change lead over that to get to the final fence. However, being on the wrong lead provides good practice for balancing the horse and coping with adverse situations.
- **Maintain the same speed** when the horse is jumping all seven (or five) of the fences in a straight line and stay in the middle of each fence.

Fixing common faults

Panicking/speeding up between fences: Refer to the previous exercise (pp. 10–11).

Knocking down fences: If the horse gets careless because the fences are small, put them up so he gives them more respect.

On landing and through the turn the rider is looking at the next fence.

Four fences on a circle

Uses
- Improves agility, speed of reactions, and the quality of the canter

Unsuitable for
- Young and inexperienced horses

This exercise works on the horse's agility and ability to maintain his balance and rhythm while turning and meeting fences that come up quickly.

SETTING UP

- Position four pairs of jump wings on a circle at three, six, nine and twelve o'clock, in the centre of the working area. Leave room to circle outside them.
- It is important that the distance is equal between each of the four fences. This is best done by marking the middle of the circle and then striding out to each fence. Ten metres (33ft, 11 paces) from the middle to each fence often works out as a good distance.

GETTING STARTED

1 Warm up on the flat. Work the horse in trot and canter on a circle both outside and inside the jump stands. The rider must maintain a rhythm and softness in the horse, while being aware that the horse is following a circular line, neither falling in nor falling out.

2 Place the poles on the floor between the jump stands and have the horse either trot or canter in a circle over them. The rider should adjust the circle so that the horse takes the same number of strides between each pole.

3 Replace the poles with uprights; use a ground line on each side. With the fences up, jump them individually in a straight line.

PROGRESSING

4 With the fences at a suitable height, starting reasonably small and building up, canter the horse on the circle, jumping the four fences. Aim to get the same number of strides between each fence.

Observe that the rider is jumping the fence in the middle and preparing for the turn as they land.

SET-UP

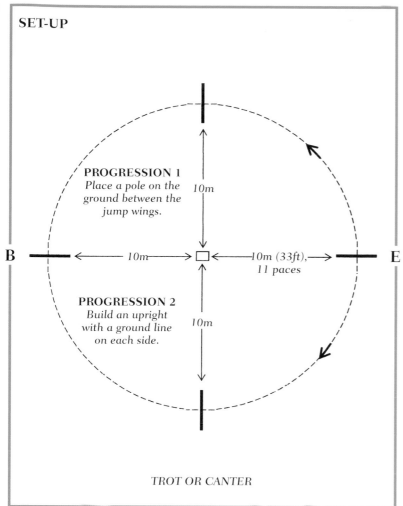

PROGRESSION 1
Place a pole on the ground between the jump wings.

10m

B ←——— 10m ———→ □ ←——10m (33ft),——→ E
                              11 paces

10m

PROGRESSION 2
Build an upright with a ground line on each side.

TROT OR CANTER

How to ride it

- **There must be harmony and rhythm between horse and rider** even if, to begin with, they find it difficult to jump and turn throughout. Linking one or two fences at a time, rather than jumping all four, may prevent this.
- **Make sure the rider maintains their balance** throughout as it is easy for them to twist to the outside. Also, ensure that the rider is controlling the outside shoulder of the horse.

Fixing common faults

Going out through the shoulder: See glossary. Use poles on the ground to help the rider control the outside shoulder if necessary.

Unable to get the same number of strides between fences: The rider has to be aware that the horse might drift out or fall in on certain parts of the circle. By anticipating this, the rider can steer a tighter or wider line between fences to help the horse maintain the same stride pattern.

Above: Place jump wings (not shown) where the fences will be built and circle outside, then inside them.

Below: Here, the rider is already looking at the next fence and preparing for the turn by guiding with the inside hand.

Fences set up as an X

Uses

■ To improve turns, balance, steering, agility and the quality of the jump

■ To develop the rider's focus

Unsuitable for

■ Horses with a low standard of flatwork

■ Riders with poor balance

This exercise works on the horse and rider's ability to turn and therefore will improve the horse's balance, manoeuvrability and agility. In addition, it will encourage the horse to be careful in his jump and to get up in the air, particularly in the last part of the exercise. It also improves the horse's canter from a jumping point of view and helps him to go on a shorter, more active stride.

At its easiest, it can be done with poles on the ground to teach riders to steer. However, the difficulty depends on the size of the working area. In a 25m-wide arena, the turns between fences will be 10–12m. If you cannot canter a circle that size without pulling the horse around it, then this exercise is too advanced for you.

SETTING UP

■ Place a block, barrel, or something similar in the middle of the school.

■ Use four poles to make an X, with a jump stand at the end of each pole.

■ Use ground lines and make the fences jumpable from either direction.

GETTING STARTED

1 As part of the warm-up, work the horse in trot and canter around the outside of the fences on the circle. Focus on the horse's rhythm and his balance, and the rider's ability to control the horse's outside shoulder.

2 Jump the arms of the X as individual fences in a straight line.

3 Jump each of the arms by jumping one arm, then make a circle back on yourself to jump the next arm, make a circle back on yourself to jump the following arm and so on, and do this on both reins.

PROGRESSING

4 Jump through the middle of the X. When jumping through the X, be prepared to lower the fences so as not to have them too big to start with, as the sloping poles encourage the horse to jump big anyway.

The horse is landing on the correct lead and horse and rider are prepared for the left turn.

Observe that the rider is in danger of losing the shoulder on the outside of the turn.

A SET UP

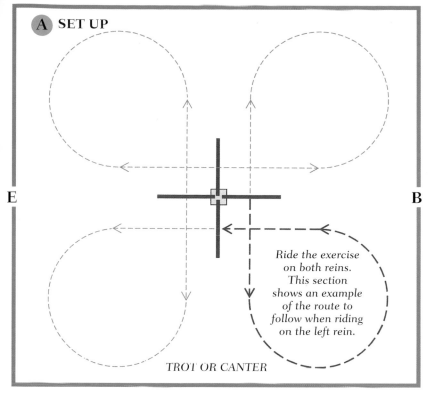

Ride the exercise on both reins. This section shows an example of the route to follow when riding on the left rein.

TROT OR CANTER

Jump one fence arm, circle, then jump the next arm.

B PROGRESSION

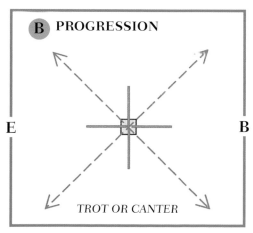

TROT OR CANTER

Jump over the centre of the X.

How to ride it

■ **Make each circle similar** in size and maintain a smoothness, rhythm and harmony in the horse.

■ **Everything can happen quite** quickly in this exercise, as you are either jumping or turning. It is important to maintain a quiet mind so you are aware of any loss of rhythm and are quick to act in the event of a poor turn. If these problems cannot be corrected as or before they happen, circle away before returning to the exercise.

Fixing common faults

One rein better than the other: Work on the horse's best rein first in order to warm the muscles more and familiarize the horse with the exercise in the easiest way. Ask only what is reasonable and reward progress immediately. Unevenness on one rein is best resolved on the flat. Be swift to sit up after the fence or your weight on his forehand will make matters worse. Opening the inside rein can help but may result in the horse falling in on the circle.

Poor rhythm: When accuracy is required, riders often resort to using too much hand, which destroys the rhythm and can result in a very choppy stride. Jump a single fence, then circle, then jump another when the rhythm has been regained.

After the turn, note that the rider has now got the horse absolutely straight for the jump.

Note that the rider is bang in the middle of the 'X'. Jumping the 'X' like this has the effect of encouraging the horse to get up in the air.

Pat Burgess

Favourite achievements

★ The first cup I ever won, and my most treasured, was for 'the most sporting rider under 12', because the pony never went anywhere near the ring! I just had to grin and bear it.

★ Gungadin was very special to me. He was a plough horse that my husband bought as a hack for £35. He had an amazing natural jump and I was devastated when David decided to sell him. Gonda Butters bought him, but she was too young to ride in adult classes so I continued to compete him until Gonda got adult status at 14. Those old enough will remember the pair of them taking on the likes of Pat Smythe, David Broome and Alan Oliver in the late 1950s.

★ Captaining the Western Province show-jumping team and beating the hot favourites, from the Transvaal, in 1958 on our home ground was just great!

Continued...

Pat Burgess was born and brought up in Cape Town, South Africa. She was show-jumping trainer to the British event team from 1980 to 1989. During that time, the team won two Olympic team silvers, an individual silver and two bronzes. They became unbeatable at the World Championships and consistently swept the board at the Europeans. Ginny Elliot, Richard Meade and Lucinda Green are among those influenced by Pat, and Lucinda still seeks her advice to this day.

Pat is the most approachable and modest of trainers, training everyone from the very great to the very novice with equal diligence and enthusiasm. Her only proviso is that her pupils must be willing to learn. In her sessions, the emphasis is on fun and doing what is best for the horse. At the age of 75, she has the energy and commitment of someone half her age and regularly teaches clinics and individual riders throughout England, and abroad.

The Riding for the Disabled Association is of enormous importance to Pat and despite being in demand as an international trainer, she devotes most of her time to teaching the disabled and increasing the opportunities available to them. Since 1975 she has been highly involved with the development of the Wilton RDA group, as a co-organizer and instructor.

Of even more importance to Pat are her five children, nine grandchildren and one great grandchild. Pat married British horse vet David Burgess in 1953 in South Africa and in 1961 they emigrated, first to Ireland, then to France and finally to England in 1964 where they settled in Salisbury (with their three children). On arrival, Pat promptly produced twins, which put paid to any more show jumping! She missed it so much she couldn't even watch it on TV. Then, in 1968, she was asked to teach at the RA Pony Club camp, which led to her training their show-jumping team, and in 1969 they qualified for Hickstead. Lucinda Prior-Palmer (Green) was in the team on her pony Sea Sway... then came Be Fair, and that is how it all started.

More... www.britisheventing.com (accredited trainers list)

Introduction to the exercises

These are some of the exercises and principles I teach at my clinics. They link together so that the horse is warmed up and stretched out, then coiled like a spring and finally opened out again with new roundness, energy, power and spring. The foundation blocks of my teaching are described under 'Fundamentals'. Refer to this before using the exercises.

Opposite, clockwise from bottom left: The Western Province Team winning the 1958 Inter-provincial in Cape Town. Pat on Taj Mahal, Gungadin being led – we tossed up to ride him! Yvonne Garrett on Drambuie and Gonda Butters on Oorskiert. (Mid far left) Pat Burgess on Gungadin in his early jumping days. (Top far left) Pat making a point. (Top centre) Amanda Barton practising the 'free hand'. (Top right) Pat, in a speed competition, showing focused intention, positive attitude and NOT a lot of style! (Mid right) Pat helping Laura Creese practise the fold. (Bottom right) Pat Burgess on Taj Mahal – still a Novice and trying his heart out at the 1958 Inter-provincial.

Favourite achievements

★ *Working with the British event team was a great privilege. I was particularly proud of their 1982 World Championship win and of Regal Realm's individual title, as so many people commented on the team's coolness under pressure and their decisive style – having only two poles down out of six rounds.*

★ *Receiving a BHS Trainer's award in 1986 was an unexpected honour.*

★ *Helping Richard Meade turn Speculator around from being a wild ride to winning Badminton in 1982 was very rewarding, especially as Lucinda Green had said 'That's one you'll never get right!'*

★ *Helping Lucinda Green with her six Badminton wins, as trainer and mentor, was also very rewarding – and great fun.*

★ *It was always a pleasure to help Ginny Elliot; she was so receptive because she was keen to be technically correct and she was always in harmony with her horses. It was very satisfying when Priceless won the World Championship at Gawler in 1986.*

TRAINING PHILOSOPHY

I really, really love horses. Every horse teaches me something and I learn something from every rider I help.

■ My passion for horses started when I was four because I was lucky enough to have a best friend who had a pony! My parents were not only non-horsey, but my father was very adamant that no daughter of his was going to do horses. He sent me to boarding school for five years to get horses out of my system but that made me even more determined to ride. As I didn't have my own pony, I rode so many different and difficult ones that I became a strong rider, although I lacked style. From when I was about 12, I spent all my holidays teaching everybody at Joan Blackwell's riding school – 14 acres of heaven! Since I wasn't allowed to go overseas and train, I had to work on my own methods and watch what other people were doing, and that made me observe and experiment. I also learnt as much as I could from books.

■ When I left school in 1948, I was helped by an Italian rider, Paulo Carpinteri, who endorsed the German Cavalry style of 'sit and grip' (I can still hear him shouting 'seet and greep')! He did not allow me to interfere with the horse at all, which made me really sit still and let the horse jump; this made me successful with many different horses – from ex-racehorses to Flemish carriage driving horses. Riding so many also gave me a deep understanding of their diverse needs during training. I took these concepts and then refined my ideas on position – by combining the Forward Seat lower leg with an upright body on the approach to a fence. This is what I teach.

■ At the heart of my philosophy is the partnership with the horse. It is so important. The horse must know that you are the boss and he must develop trust and confidence in you, and respect for you. People try to establish their dominance with whips, strong bits and so on, but it is not that at all. This is why I like both the Natural Horsemanship and Intelligent Horsemanship approach; the horse learns to respect and bond with their rider on the ground first. I get really upset when the horse is ridden badly or just used and abused to gratify the rider's ego.

■ The partnership must be built on trust, mutual respect and discipline. You must have an affinity with the horse – a love and understanding of him. A true 'horse-man' achieves the perfect partnership by becoming one with his horse on every level: physical, mental, emotional and spiritual. To achieve that bond you must be finely tuned to each other, using your body language and thoughts to communicate instinctively. That harmony is the difference between mediocrity and brilliance. The horse has to want to jump, it has to be his choice – but you make it his choice through your intention becoming his intention. This will only happen if you progress slowly so that the work is easy and you build his confidence – it cannot happen by force.

■ My main priorities are for the horse to be balanced in front of the fence and to have the freedom to jump. The rider must sit up, sit light, sit still and wait for the horse to lift off before they fold from the hips and free the reins. They must have the security to be able to stay in balance and be independent of the reins. This is why the main thing I teach riders is the importance of the 'Jumping Lower Leg': it allows them to fold deeply and move the hand forwards, giving the horse maximum freedom in the air. This keeps the horse happy because it allows him to use his full scope and enjoy his jump. I watch the horse's eye to see if he is enjoying jumping – and if not, why not? Every horse is different – is he happy, soft and focused or anxious, panicky or stubborn? I mentally ride every horse I teach and get a big thrill when they go well. That is why I love teaching.

ADVICE TO NEWCOMERS

Establish your Jumping Lower Leg. Plug in your seat bones and sit up!

Partnership: *Lucinda Green showing her perfect partnership with Miss De Meena.*

A good rider position in the air. *She has a flat back, her head is up, and her heel down. The rider has total security in the leg and a free, soft, light hand that allows the horse to stretch. The horse is not basculing in the air, possibly because the jump is small for its level of training.*

A good bascule. *The rider is allowing the horse to use its head and neck to bascule and although her leg has come too far back, she is still in balance. This is an example of over-freeing the hand for the horse to really learn to stretch; this horse was in need of opening out at the start of the session and was still learning to find its balance. The next stage is to maintain a contact while keeping that stretch.*

Pat Burgess

Fundamentals

These exercises and concepts will help you to achieve a harmonious partnership with your horse. The aim is to increase your awareness of how you ride and how you treat your horse. Being aware of what you do gives you the chance to improve it, using the left (learning) side of your brain. Once you are doing the correct things regularly, they become habits and therefore automatic. It is these habits, stored in the right (subconscious) side of your brain, which you revert to whenever you react instinctively. Once the body and the mind are programmed with the correct technique, then you can react positively to whatever your horse does.

GETTING STARTED

1 **Breathing exercise:** Start every session by using 'Conscious Breathing' (see box at right). This is an invaluable method of releasing tension from you and your horse.

2 **The voice and transitions to halt:** After the breathing exercise, work on walk-to-halt transitions. See box at right.

3 **Position:** Your position provides the foundations on which you build your jumping skills (see 'Position', p.24). Check that your legs are in the correct place with your weight dropping down through the heel, at the start of every jumping session and periodically throughout it.

4 **RIBS WITH LOVE FROM PAT:** This is an acronym for everything to consider when riding a course (see p.23). Pick out the things that you do WELL and visualize doing them. Then think about each of the other concepts in turn and work to improve one or two things at a time. Every time you do something well, you are programming your body in the right way.

PROGRESSING

5 Work to become more and more conscious of how your horse is going and how you are riding. Eventually you will develop an automatic feel for your horse being in balance with sufficient impulsion, a strong, round, medium-length stride and a good rhythm at the right speed. You will correct any deviation from that without conscious thought. Your position and attitude will encompass all the points listed opposite and it will all be a matter of habit. Then you are truly free to think about whatever crops up as the priority of the moment, such as getting the line right and preventing problems before they occur.

6 Doing the right thing is only helpful if your reactions are quick enough. Improve the speed of your reactions by doing exercises that specifically work on them.

The voice

Use your voice to communicate quietly with your horse; 'whoa' can be shortened to 'ho', said in a short, quiet way to get the horse's attention. It can be used as an additional aid to slow the horse or to assist any downward transition. The voice should be introduced early on in the horse's training and used throughout all the exercises.

Breathing exercise

- Start in walk and breathe in for a number of strides then out for the same number, releasing any tension out down your arms on the outward breath. Breathe in calm and breathe it out to your horse. Breathe in love and breathe it out to your horse. Breathe rhythm into him.
- Move on into a slow trot, and find your own timing. Try breathing in for four strides and out for five, for example. Count as you sit. Use a short rein with a long arm, soft hand and soft elbows.
- Conscious Breathing establishes rhythm and promotes a sense of calm in horse and rider. It is very helpful in releasing the tension created in the back of the neck and through the arms by, for example, driving a lorry on the way to an event. Practised every day, eventually the technique becomes automatic and as you start the breathing, so the horse starts relaxing as well.

Transitions to halt

- Visualize the horse doing a perfect four-square halt. Breathe out and softly say 'whoa' or 'ho' in conjunction with your other aids. As soon as he halts, soften your fingers and immediately reward him by scratching or rubbing him in front of and beside his withers – LOVE him!
- This method of reward allows you to maintain your position and therefore does not disturb the horse's balance. Horses often groom each other like this out at grass and it has been proven to lower their heart rate. Through repetition, the horse will link your 'whoa' or 'ho' to this sensation. This phenomenon is called 'neuro-association through pleasure'. Once the link is established, whenever you softly say 'whoa' or 'ho' your horse will very quickly become calm and pay attention to you.

Fixing common faults

The worst faults are getting in front of the movement, losing the lower leg position in the air (see 'Opening out the horse', p.30), and restricting the horse's freedom in the air (see 'The rein contact', p.25).

'RIBS WITH LOVE FROM PAT'

R

	RESPECT	Your horse must respect **you** as the alpha, the leader in the partnership, and you must respect **him**.
	RHYTHM	Keep the rhythm in the stride.
	RIDE	Ride every stride, especially around the turns.
	RELEASE	Use the crest-release technique as the horse jumps (see p.25).

I

IMPULSION Legs, legs, legs until lift off. So often, when the horse does not have a stride, instead of riding on, riders freeze, and just when the horse needs more energy and extra confidence, he gets less. Or, they ride on 'presumption'. That is, when the stride is good, they stop riding and the horse stops.

INTENTION Your intention (about where you are going) must be strong enough that the horse picks it up. Never take 'time out' by looking at the ground or the horse as that gives him the chance to nap to the collecting ring or do whatever he wants to do (such as run out!).

B

BALANCE Sit up straight until you get to the jump so that you maintain the balance.

BEAM Beam at the jump. Create a line of thought energy from you, through the horse's mind to the jump.

BREATHE! Don't hold your breath – your body needs oxygen! Breathe out to release neck and shoulder tension.

BACK THE BODY Back the body off the fence. Sit up for security in front of the fence so that you don't fall off if he stops and to enable you to use your legs better. Try using your legs while leaning forwards – it is very difficult.

BELIEVE Believe in yourself and your horse, and you will 'Achieve'.

S

STRETCH Allow the horse to stretch in the air so that he can reach the full potential of his jump.

SECURITY To free the hand in the air, you must feel safe. You will only feel safe if the lower leg stays secure, no matter what happens. Think 'lower leg – security' (see 'The Jumping Lower Leg, p.24).

SUPPLE HIP To stay with the horse you must be quick to fold from the hip and not from the waist.

SOFTNESS Stay soft in the hands and elbows. The horse will not be happy to stretch in the air if the hand is hard (see 'The rein contact', p.25).

SYMPATHY Empathize with your horse and strive to understand him. If you have no empathy with him, your aids will be mechanical and unsympathetic. His response to you will be the same.

SHOULDERS Shoulders back. The smallest movement can make a huge difference to the horse's balance.

STRIDE The stride must be of medium length so that it can be shortened or lengthened as necessary on the approach.

SPEED The speed must be the right speed for the horse and for the course.

SIT STILL Sit still before the jump.

SEAT BONES The seat bones must be lightly 'plugged' into the saddle and not 'unplugged' until lift-off (see 'The seat', p.24).

SELF-ESTEEM Stay positive and don't beat yourself up if you make a mistake.

SELF-CONTROL Discipline yourself never to allow fear, frustration or anger to take over.

W

(I)

TH

WAIT Train your body to wait for the jump – do not move from the vertical until you feel the take-off, or you will unbalance the horse, causing him to put in an extra stride (see 'Getting in front of the movement', p.30).

THINK FAST Think fast and do not allow yourself 'time out', and never think back.

LOVE

Love your horse! ... and he must love your hands

F

FOCUS Focus at the jump, and the next and the next ...

FOLD Fold from the hips.

FEEL Feel what the horse is telling you, through your seat bones; feel if he is taking off or putting in another stride.

FORWARDS Keep riding forwards to the jump.

FR

FREEDOM Give the horse freedom in the air.

FRONT Keep the horse in front of you to keep him balanced.

O

ORGANIZE Be organized.

OBEDIENCE The horse must totally respect your commands and be instantly obedient to the aids. This can only be achieved by work on the flat.

M

MIND Thought is a form of energy. Direct this energy powerfully into your intention.
Mentally rehearse. While you are with your horse, visualize the perfect round and transmit this to him as a series of mental pictures. He will see your thoughts and your round will go more smoothly as a result.

P

AT

POSITIVE ATTITUDE: If your mind is positive, your body is energized. Tell yourself 'I **can** do it!'.

PAY ATTENTION Pay attention to your horse's needs; be aware of what he is doing and how he is feeling.

PARTNER 'SHIP' There must be a perfect partnership between horse and rider.

I must be the captain of my 'ship', my body and mind are the crew and under my control.

Position

THE SEAT

Think of plugging your seat bones into the saddle like two plugs into two sockets. Then you are connected lightly to the horse and can really FEEL what he is doing. The connection may be deep at times but must never be heavy. Do not unplug until take-off. You must only sit and drive with your seat and back when your horse is really going to stop. The main aids for impulsion are the legs.

Plugged in on the approach to a jump.

THE FORWARD SEAT

The (unplugged) Forward Seat has the great advantage of freeing the horse's back muscles, but carries a risk of unbalancing him in front of the fence if it is not used correctly. For example, if the horse 'props', you may not be able to stop yourself from falling forwards, whereas if you are sitting up then you will be pushed deeper, into a driving position, in this situation. Essentially, you need to be strong in the lower leg to use this seat – which is why men, with their powerful long strong legs, can adopt it successfully. The Forward Seat is the *ultimate* in perfection but requires the rider to be very quick to sit up if there is a problem and to be sufficiently strong with their legs when necessary, despite being forwards.

THE JUMPING LOWER LEG

To be independent of the reins, every rider needs to have a lower leg that does not move when they are in the air. The leg must not move even a millimetre out of position. In other words, it must be 100% secure to allow the horse 100% freedom over the fence. That security is gained from 60% gravity and 40% grip. For the leg to be solidly anchored, the stirrup leather must remain vertical so that the rider's centre of gravity is through the heel. The joints work like shock absorbers with the weight sinking through the knee, ankle, ball of the foot and heel like a

soft spring. The stirrup acts as a fulcrum with the rider's weight through the heel counterbalancing the forward fold of the body and the free hands. The grip is a sinking grip using the top third of the calf, below the knee. If the rider over-grips with the knee and thigh, the weight cannot travel downwards and the leg swings back (see 'Losing the lower leg position', p.30).

For every rider's leg there is an ideal stirrup length where the angle of the thigh is at 45 degrees to a right-angle at the hip (see photo). This provides the optimum support for the body and makes the dynamics of the weight through the leg correct.

Put the stirrup on the ball of the foot, and the foot on the inside of the stirrup. With the horse at 12 o'clock as you look down, turn the left foot out to five to twelve and the right foot out to five past twelve. Relax the ankle enough to let the weight drop through to the heel. If the feet are parallel to the horse, the ankle is blocked and the weight cannot sink down to the heel. Without the weight anchored in the heel, you may not be able to give the horse full freedom over the fence.

Right: The correct leg position: the rider's weight is going down to the heel to counterbalance the free hand, and the thigh is at a 45-degree angle to a right-angle at the hip.

THE FOLD

For show jumping, the fold must be from the hip joint. If it is from the waist, with the pelvic girdle remaining upright, the rider gets behind the movement causing the horse to knock rails down behind. However, for cross-country, folding from the waist is permissible because it gives a good defensive position. I do not

The rider is practising the fold from the hip and the crest release. When the horse is in the air the hands would go further forwards, however the rider is showing the correct way to practise the fold at halt. The head is up so that the back muscles hold the body. The weight is in the heel and not on the hands.

object to a deep fold, provided that the rider's weight remains through the heel and not on the neck. It is important to practise folding without fences, to speed your progress and reduce the risk of faults creeping in while you improve. Start in halt, then practise in trot. Fold smoothly and swiftly, taking care to keep the lower leg absolutely still and the leather vertical, with the foot pressing firmly on the stirrup so the weight goes down through the heel.

THE CREST-RELEASE TECHNIQUE

Move the hands up the neck on top of the crest as you fold over the fence. Keep the weight in the heel, NEVER on the hands. Do not throw your hands up the neck; the hands and elbows must stay soft so that it is a smooth release, giving the horse maximum freedom over the fence. Although it is correct to make a straight line from the elbow, through the wrist to the bit, it is very difficult for the rider to give enough while keeping their balance. Therefore, for the sake of both horse and rider, I teach the crest-release technique even to more experienced riders.

THE REIN CONTACT

A lot of horses never reach their full potential as jumpers because of the rider's contact. When the contact is too strong and the hand is hard, the horse will resist it, causing his neck muscles to tighten. This then means he cannot get his knees up to jump, nor stay balanced in the air, nor stretch to get his hind legs up. This can cause a knock-down in show jumping or a fall across country. For the horse to be happy to take the hand and stretch, he has to feel softness in the contact. The risk of teaching novice riders to jump on a contact is that instead of relying on their legs for security they learn to balance on their reins. I encourage novice riders who are insecure in their leg, to hold the mane halfway up the crest, so that the horse can jump well, allowing the rider to work on their position. The strength of the rein contact varies according to the individual horse, his stage of training and his own preference.

Above: This is a novice horse being given the freedom to be able to work out what to do with its legs without the rider interfering. The rider's security is in the leg, and the angles at the ankle, knee and hip are correct.

Right: A restricted take-off. Instead of folding, the rider has brought herself up into this position using her hands.

Far right: A restricted landing. The rider has got left behind and is not allowing the horse freedom on landing.

Below: The rider is with the horse's movement, coming back slowly into an upright position allowing the horse to finish its jump. She has perfect security in the leg with the seat coming softly into the saddle.

Warming up: stretching the horse

Uses
- For self-carriage
- For stretching stiff muscles and ligaments

Unsuitable for
- Both exercises are suitable for most horses and riders

These two exercises can be done together: one on each long side. They help to identify and release any stiffness in the horse, free him laterally and improve his ability to carry himself. They strengthen the lines of communication between the horse and rider. Start by doing the breathing exercise and transitions to halt (p.22).

Bending through poles on the ground

This exercise warms up the horse, mentally and physically, before starting work. The poles ask the horse to bend while being far enough apart to keep him thinking forwards. This leaves the rider free to guide the horse primarily with their focus and intention, developing the use of subtle aids. The effect that your thoughts and general state of mind have on the horse cannot be overstated. It is of huge benefit to be able to use minimal aids to explain what you want the horse to do, particularly as the fences become more complex through his career.

SETTING UP

- Place the poles in a straight line about 5m (16½ft) off the track.

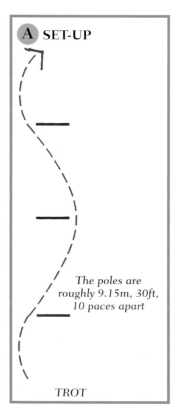

A SET-UP

The poles are roughly 9.15m, 30ft, 10 paces apart

TROT

Guide the horse around them in sweeping curves on both reins.

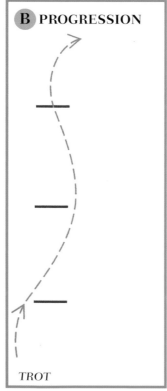

B PROGRESSION

TROT

Trot over the centre of the final pole without altering the rhythm. Do the same on both reins.

Right: This is what you are aiming for.

GETTING STARTED

1 Follow the route shown in diagram A, in trot. Place the poles far enough apart that the exercise can be done without the need for strong aids.

2 Ride over the middle of the final pole (diagram B). This checks that the horse will trot calmly over a pole and is alert and responsive to a change in instructions. It also varies the exercise. Again, work on both reins, trotting over the last pole.

How to ride it
- **Use the power of your intention** to help guide the horse through the poles.
- **Keep your head up and look where you are going** – do not look at the poles.
- **Steer the horse mainly with your legs** and make the turns smooth using a very soft hand.

Trotting poles on a turn

The main purpose of this exercise is to release any stiffness in the horse, stretch him out and get him to carry himself. Most horses are stiff on one side so you are working to release that stiffness through stretching. This is similar in effect to you touching your toes – after each attempt you can stretch further. The exercise starts moving the horse's hocks underneath him, which is essential for jumping and teaches him to carry himself instead of the rider carrying him.

SETTING UP

■ Place seven poles, with guide rails, on a 25–30m (82–89½ft) circle.

■ Do not place the poles on too tight a curve.

How to ride it

■ **Keep the pace slow.** Trot into the poles in a slow rhythm so that you can give the horse the freedom he needs as he goes over them. Use Conscious Breathing and do not allow him to rush.

■ **Let the horse see the task.** Use a soft rein and make sure that he sees what he has to do before he meets the first pole.

■ **Beam into the poles.** Allow your peripheral vision to see the circle but focus slightly downwards to guide the horse into the poles.

■ **Allow the horse to carry himself.** Free the hands forwards and keep them soft so he can stretch as much as he needs to. It is especially important to release the outside rein.

■ **Feel his back come up.** Feel him asking for the rein to stretch. Allow him to put his head right out and down. Feel his tension releasing, his hocks working and, most importantly, his back come up underneath you. Feel his shoulders releasing and if he starts to lick and chew, that means he's 'all yours!'. The softer you are, the softer your horse will be. Remember, it takes two to fight, so drop out of the fight. Breathe calm into him.

Fixing common faults

Most people want to carry their horses and hold them too tightly: you must be independent of the reins to allow the horse to stretch so he carries himself. You must control the rhythm and pace of the trot around the circle so it does not change through the poles as the hand moves forward. Use your soft 'ho' if he starts to rush.

Distances

All distances are approximate – all must be tailored to the individual horse's length of stride and the height of the fences. The measurements here are for horses between 15.2 and 16.2hh.

GETTING STARTED

1 This exercise can be done with, after, or instead of the 'Bending through poles' exercise. The horse must already be happy and relaxed with two or three trotting poles in a straight line.

2 Work over the centre of the poles and make sure that you establish a constant rhythm.

PROGRESSING

3 Move the inner guide rails towards the middle of the poles to send the horse on to their outer edge. This causes him to take longer strides and become more free in his movement. His back should begin to swing.

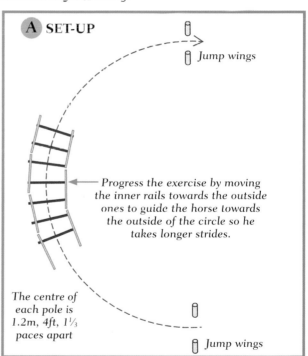

A SET-UP

Jump wings

Progress the exercise by moving the inner rails towards the outside ones to guide the horse towards the outside of the circle so he takes longer strides.

The centre of each pole is 1.2m, 4ft, 1⅓ paces apart

Jump wings

Below: This is nice in that the horse is relaxed and happy. He has a free rein and is just starting to take it to stretch.

Place seven poles on a 25–30m (82–98½ft) circle. Do not make the curve too tight. Position guide rails as shown, altering them to suit the rein you are on.

Below: Place either ordinary poles or narrower batons on top of the trotting poles to help guide the horse. Tilt them away from the direction of travel.

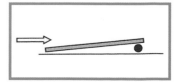

Bounces on a turn: coiling the spring

Uses

■ Teaches the horse to think fast, pat the ground, shorten, and snap up his legs

■ Improves agility, steering, and horse and rider confidence and technique

Unsuitable for

■ Horses or riders that are not confident over single fences or that are unable to stay in balance after them

Bounces help to develop the horse's reflexes; they make him snap up his front legs quickly, shorten his stride and help him to develop a good rounded jump. They encourage him to ping off the ground with both hind legs together and really develop the technique of his jump so he gets a more active jump. The exercise as a whole stretches the horse's top line and improves the canter, because with the top line stretched the hocks can come further underneath the horse. Jumping on a turn helps to get the rider focused and makes them use their outside leg. It also stretches the horse's stiff side, helping to make him more supple. Horses become much softer through this exercise as their responses become automatic through the repetition of the work. It helps them to find their rhythm and confidence and teaches them to think fast.

SETTING UP

■ Place a cross pole on a 25–30m (82–98½ft) circle with ground poles before and after it (see diagram A).
■ Use jump wings and guide rails to help the horse onto the right line before and after the fence.
■ Place ground poles before and after the cross-pole fence (see diagram A).

GETTING STARTED

1 Warm up by using the breathing exercise and transitions to halt (p.22), then do the stretching exercises on p.26.

2 Approach the grid in trot. After it, maintain the canter and look up to guide the horse through the empty wings and around a circle. Come back to trot to repeat the exercise, usually about three times. Then do the same on the other rein. If your horse is rushing, bring him back to trot earlier.

3 Keep the fence small in order to concentrate on the rhythm.

PROGRESSING

4 Add fences as shown on diagram B. I never put a bounce in a grid without first having cantered over a pole on the ground – hence the ground poles. These are gradually replaced by jumps so that the canter stride over the pole naturally progresses to a jump. The rhythm should not alter because of the additional fences. You are working towards a more active horse.

5 Change the rein and add more fences (diagram C). Depending on your horse's stride and stage of training, you can now start approaching the grid in canter. Keep a short-striding canter all the way to the final upright.

6 Change the rein again and add two more cross poles to make a fourth bounce (diagram D).

7 At this point, there are various options for progressing further: you can raise the fences to demand more athleticism; make the final upright more spooky or narrower to test obedience and rider reactions; or leave the distances the same but ask for more or less strides to test obedience, lengthening and shortening.

8 The grid MUST be straightened out at the end, whether or not you do the next exercise.

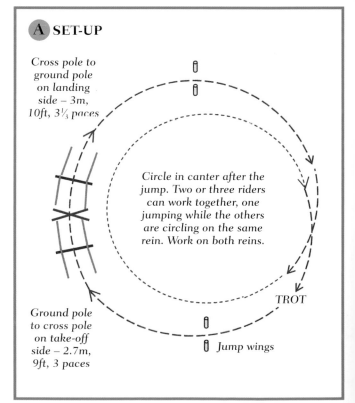

A SET-UP

Cross pole to ground pole on landing side – 3m, 10ft, 3⅓ paces

Circle in canter after the jump. Two or three riders can work together, one jumping while the others are circling on the same rein. Work on both reins.

TROT

Ground pole to cross pole on take-off side – 2.7m, 9ft, 3 paces

Jump wings

Place a cross pole on a 25–30m (82–98½ft) circle. Use jump wings to guide the horse onto the right line before and after the grid. Do not make the curve of the grid too tight.

How to ride it

■ **Look up and focus your attention at each jump.** As you go over each fence, focus on the next while 'staying in the now' for the one you are actually jumping or you risk hitting it. Maintain your concentration all the way to the upright after the last bounce. Focus your attention on each jump as well as having peripheral vision of the whole circle.

■ **Keep your seat lightly in the saddle and flow with the movement through the bounces.** Feel like you are a rubber dinghy flowing down a river in rapids (the horse is the river). Sit up in between the fences and use your 'whoa' if the horse is rushing (see 'The voice', p.22).

■ **Control the turn.** Sit up and use the outside leg to stop the horse from falling out, to keep him coming forwards and to make him use his inside hock. Use the inside leg into the outside hand to prevent him from falling in. The inside leg maintains the energy through the turn and the outside rein regulates the power. Don't switch off after the last bounce! Keep your focus and ride the turn correctly.

■ **Keep the horse in front of you.** Do not lean forwards until he takes off.

■ **Keep the pace constant.** As the exercise becomes more testing, it is increasingly important to approach with sufficient impulsion and maintain it throughout the entire grid. The speed should remain constant through the grid and around the arena.

Fixing common faults

Drifting to the outside: Bring the guide rails in a little to encourage the horse to the centre.

Ground lines

Place a pole on the ground either side of each fence in all grids. Rake the take-off and landing areas frequently for all grid-work.

Jump cups

Remove any unused cups from the jump wings for safety. Take care not to abandon any cups on the floor when moving the wings.

Distances

All distances are approximate. These measurements are for horses between 15.2 and 16.2hh. However, all must be tailored to the individual horse's length of stride and the height of the fences.

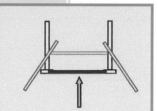

Refer to the previous exercise and use guide rails for all progressions. Guide rails must slope away from the direction of travel. They can be angled up on to the last fence of the grid.

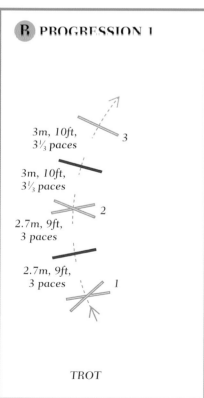

B PROGRESSION 1

3m, 10ft, 3⅓ paces — 3

3m, 10ft, 3⅓ paces

2.7m, 9ft, 3 paces — 2

2.7m, 9ft, 3 paces — 1

TROT

Add a cross pole and an upright each a stride away at either end of the grid. Check that the crosses line up around the curve by standing on the line of approach.

C PROGRESSION 2

TROT OR CANTER

3m, 10ft, 3⅓ paces — 1

3m, 10ft, 3⅓ paces — 2

3m, 10ft, 3⅓ paces — 3

3m, 10ft, 3⅓ paces — 4

3 strides, 13.7m, 45ft, 15 paces

5

Change the rein and add another cross and, three strides away from the grid, an upright. From this point on, the more experienced can approach from a short, bouncy canter.

D PROGRESSION 3

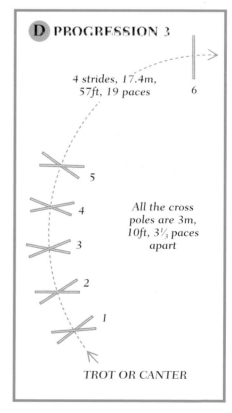

4 strides, 17.4m, 57ft, 19 paces — 6

5

4

All the cross poles are 3m, 10ft, 3⅓ paces apart

3

2

1

TROT OR CANTER

Change the rein and make the grid into four bounces. Remove what was fence 5 (diagram C) and ride through the wings again.

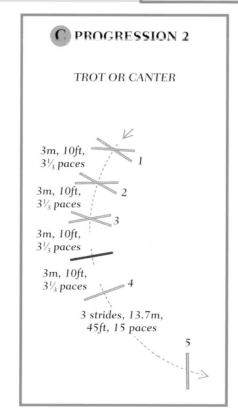
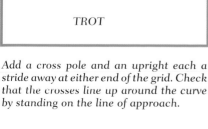
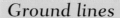

Opening out the horse

Pat Burgess

Uses
- Agility, straightness and maintenance of natural bascule
- Improves horse and rider's jumping technique and confidence

Unsuitable for
- Horses that are unable to go forwards and straight
- Horses or riders unable to stay in reasonable balance through a grid
- The horse must be confident over bounce fences before doing this exercise

The horse's natural jump can suffer as a result of the demands of competition. This grid helps to stretch him out again so that he uses the entire length of his back and neck over the fence. Releasing his neck muscles frees his shoulders, enabling him to snap up his front legs so he jumps neatly and carefully. I find this exercise particularly suitable for more experienced horses. For novice horses or riders, I would use a more simple grid than this one.

This exercise should be done after the previous ones ('Stretching out the horse' and 'Bounces on a turn').

SETTING UP

- Set up a grid with cross poles and ground poles (see diagram A). If you are progressing from the previous exercises, start with three cross poles. Otherwise, begin with the first cross alone and add ground poles one at a time where the other crosses will be. The oxer is added later.
- Place the fences off the track and allow sufficient space for several strides after the grid so that the horse can halt comfortably after the oxer, once that is added. Use guide rails – shown in brown. Refer to the previous exercises to see how to use them.

GETTING STARTED

1 If you have not done the preceding exercises, warm up using the breathing exercise and transitions to halt (p.22). Build up the grid gradually adding one bounce at a time.

2 If you have just completed the previous exercise, start with the bounces and then add the oxer. It is important to maintain the energy after the bounces so that the stride to the oxer stays round.

3 After the oxer, bring the horse to a halt at the end of the arena – for discipline. Use your voice, out breath and reward, as well as your normal aids for halt. Place a marker to focus on at the end of the arena.

How to ride it
- **Before the oxer, coil the spring** like a jack-in-a box, by using your legs to bring the hocks into your hands. Then bring your shoulders back and soften your hands to release the jack-in-a box and allow the jump. Be aware that every horse is different. Some horses prefer a strong contact on take-off and throughout the jump whereas others prefer a release of contact.
- **For riding the halt** refer to 'The voice' and 'Transitions to halt', p.22.

Fixing common faults

Sitting heavily in front of the oxer: There is a temptation to ride with the seat and sit heavily as the oxer gets bigger. This will cause the horse to hollow and hit the front bar. Be aware of this and sit lighter in the last stride. Create impulsion through the legs, not the seat, by really wrapping the legs in, coiling the spring and then releasing it.

Rider getting in front of the movement: The worst fault is to unbalance the horse in front of the jump by unplugging and tipping forwards before take-off. This can result in a fall across country as the horse tries to put in an extra stride to regain his balance and finds there is no space for it. Since he is already over his point of balance, he falls. In show jumping, it may cause him to knock down the front pole. The horse must feel confident that you will not get in front of the movement, otherwise he may habitually put in an extra stride as a defensive measure. It is vital to keep the weight in the heel, back the body off the fence and wait for the jump. Note that being in front of the movement is not the same thing as being in the Forward Seat.

Losing the lower leg position in the air: The biggest thing to avoid is movement of the lower leg. If the rider over-grips with the thigh and knee, and pivots on the knee, the lower leg will swing back and move their centre of gravity forwards. As they lose balance, they look for security in the hands and this prevents them from giving the horse the freedom he needs in the air. This can result in the back pole falling or, worse, can cause the horse to fall across country. To correct this fault, practise folding when you are not jumping and pay particular attention to your weight remaining in the heel, with your feet positioned at five to one. Make sure your stirrups are the correct length (see 'The Jumping Lower Leg', p.24).

A SET-UP

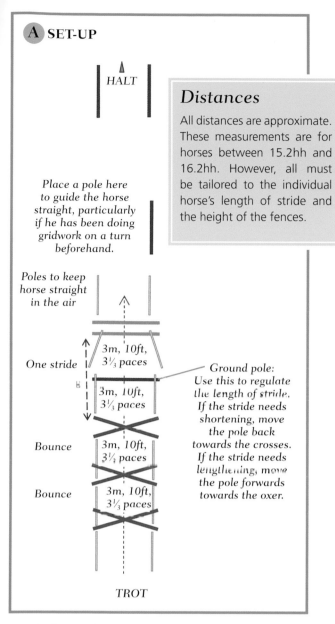

HALT

Place a pole here to guide the horse straight, particularly if he has been doing gridwork on a turn beforehand.

Distances

All distances are approximate. These measurements are for horses between 15.2hh and 16.2hh. However, all must be tailored to the individual horse's length of stride and the height of the fences.

Poles to keep horse straight in the air

One stride — 3m, 10ft, 3⅓ paces

Ground pole: Use this to regulate the length of stride. If the stride needs shortening, move the pole back towards the crosses. If the stride needs lengthening, move the pole forwards towards the oxer.

3m, 10ft, 3⅓ paces

Bounce — 3m, 10ft, 3⅓ paces

Bounce — 3m, 10ft, 3⅓ paces

TROT

Set the fences off the track. Make sure all the crosses line up with a cone or block at the end of the arena. This is where you will halt.

B PROGRESSIONS

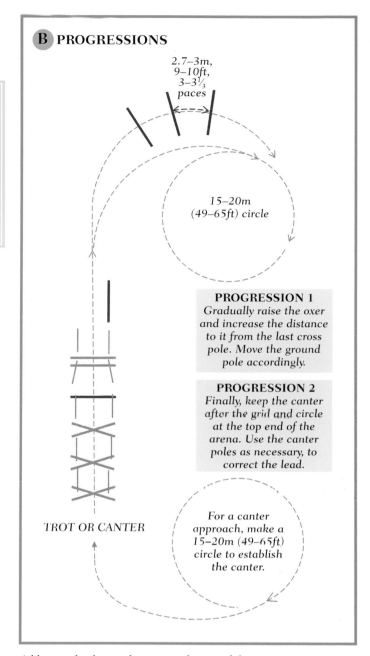

2.7–3m, 9–10ft, 3–3⅓ paces

15–20m (49–65ft) circle

PROGRESSION 1
Gradually raise the oxer and increase the distance to it from the last cross pole. Move the ground pole accordingly.

PROGRESSION 2
Finally, keep the canter after the grid and circle at the top end of the arena. Use the canter poles as necessary, to correct the lead.

TROT OR CANTER

For a canter approach, make a 15–20m (49–65ft) circle to establish the canter.

Add ground poles on the turn at the top of the arena.

PROGRESSING

4 When you are jumping confidently and achieving a good halt, raise and spread the oxer (parallel). Use your discretion as to whether it is ascending or square. At the same time, raise the bounces to get the horse up (so there is more height in his bascule). Increase the distance to the oxer as the fences get higher, according to how your horse is jumping. If the distance is too long, the stride may become flat and the value of the exercise will be lost.

5 If your horse's stage of training allows, approach the grid in canter (diagram B).

6 The next stage is to keep the canter after the grid and circle at the top end of the arena.

7 Place three poles on the turn at the top. **If the lead is wrong** and the horse's balance is good enough, using the poles will change the lead and help teach him flying changes. If it is wrong and that unbalances him, change through trot, using 'ho' and avoiding the poles (see 'The voice, p.22). **If the lead is correct,** avoid the poles.

8 Watch horses jumping without a rider to see how they use themselves. When teaching, observe how easy or hard the horse finds it to stretch over the fence. Notice whether he is neat with his legs or not and how much he springs from his hocks.

AND FINALLY...

After the gridwork, when you are happy with your own and your horse's technique and are working in partnership, set up a small course. This is 'PLAYTIME' – practise 'Ribs with love from Pat'.

Have fun and GOOD LUCK!

Karen Dixon MBE

Favourite achievements

★My first ride round Badminton aged 18 on Running Bear was special because I was one of the youngest competitors. He was a special horse to me as I had retrained him from racing to eventing.

★Winning the individual bronze and team gold medal at the World Championships in 1994 on Get Smart was fantastic for that horse. Having achieved so much with him, it was the icing on the cake.

★I had a baby in the spring of 1999 and returned to top level, coming second to Mark Todd at Burghley – but finishing on equal points. Although it was frustrating not to win, it was a fantastic result considering I had a 6-month-old baby!

Karen is an Olympic team silver medallist who has represented Britain at four Olympic Games. Her achievements include winning a team gold, team silver and an individual bronze for Britain over three World Championships. She holds two British Open titles and won team gold at two European Championships, also winning individual bronze at Punchestown. She is still one of the youngest people ever to ride round Badminton and has often been in the top ten there and at Burghley. Karen is Senior Trainer at Queen Ethelburga's College and lives in County Durham.

More… www.britisheventing.com (accredited trainer's list)

TRAINING PHILOSOPHY

■ When training a young horse, I try to build a solid foundation and if anything goes wrong, I go straight back to that foundation. That is the base from which I build. With a young horse I will be doing exercises every single day, broadening his education, building his confidence and developing a partnership with him. With the older horses, exercises provide a bit of variety to keep their interest in the training. I will use some gridwork or lunge jumping between their other work, be that galloping, dressage lessons or whatever they are doing that week.

ADVICE TO NEWCOMERS

■ 'Don't try and look for a stride, ride the canter.' Have a positive, active canter that the horse can jump from and just continue to ride that canter, rather than looking for a stride. With a good canter, the horse can take off from anywhere. When I am jumping I say to myself 'rhythm and balance, rhythm and balance' so I stay in a good rhythm to the fence.

Introduction to the exercises

The following exercises are the ones that I use regularly, and which I believe educate horses and build their confidence.

Random poles

Uses
- Improves canter rhythm, balance and rider's focus
- Speeds reactions, adds variety, encourages activity
- Improves rider's seat (ability to absorb movement and sit still) and develops steering

Unsuitable for
- This exercise suits most horses and riders

This exercise improves the canter, by encouraging the horse to maintain a calm, even rhythm with a medium stride length. It develops the horse's ability to think for himself and cope with the unexpected so he meets each pole 'right' and gives the rider a comfortable ride. Plus, it teaches the rider to sit still and quietly without trying to look for a stride.

When it is ridden at walk and trot, it can be used to familiarize a young horse, or inexperienced rider, with poles. In addition, it can add variety to a more experienced horse's work and encourage him to be more active.

Finally, this is a great exercise for teaching riders to steer effectively, at any pace.

How to ride it

- **In all paces, plan each turn** and look well ahead to make certain the horse has time to see the poles.

- **Let the horse stretch forwards** over the poles.

- **Use frequent half-halts** to help maintain balance, but do not use them while going over a pole.

- **When changing the rein in canter,** it is easiest to make a flying change over a pole. If your horse is not ready to do this, change the rein through trot away from the poles.

- **Maintain rhythm and balance** round the course of poles and make full use of the arena and its corners. You are aiming for a comfortable ride during which you hardly notice the poles are there. If you can ride poles well, you will ride fences well. So, when you replace the poles with fences and ride a course, you will have a good round.

Fixing common faults

Lurching and propping over the poles: If this is because the horse's canter is unbalanced and not rhythmic, use circles and transitions to improve it before returning to the exercise. If he is spooking, return to walk and add a few extra poles, to help him overcome his fears through repetition.

Tripping over the poles: Look where you are going and allow the horse to see what he is doing. Maintain rhythm and balance to the poles; riders frequently either hold too much or put the leg on and speed up in front of the poles. Both these faults can cause the horse to trip as he goes over them.

SETTING UP

- This exercise is harder than it looks. If you are on your own, it is tempting to put many poles out before you start. However, using just two or three poles (see diagram A) ensures there is plenty of space for circling to re-establish the canter.
- When adding poles, place them a minimum of 4.6m (15ft), or five paces, apart so the horse has time to adjust his stride.

GETTING STARTED

1 Depending on how you are going to use the exercise, ride over one or two poles in walk, trot and canter, as part of your warm-up. From the saddle, it is easier to decide where it is feasible to place any more poles. At the same time, you can gauge your horse's reaction to them. Even experienced horses can baulk at a pole on the ground, if they have only ever been presented with fences.

2 Keep the horse fresh by cantering large around the arena from time to time.

PROGRESSING

3 When you can keep a constant rhythm and even stride over a few poles, introduce some more difficult turns (diagram B). The turns will help to collect the canter.

4 Add some poles within a few strides of each other, without measuring the distance between them (diagram C). This further tests your horse's ability to adjust his stride quickly and effortlessly.

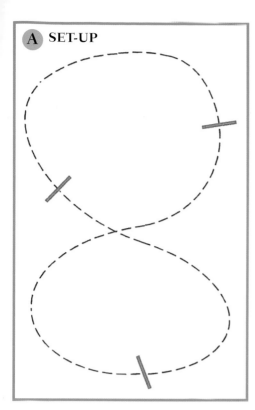

A SET-UP

Start with a few poles, well spread out around the arena, and make sweeping turns and circles between them.

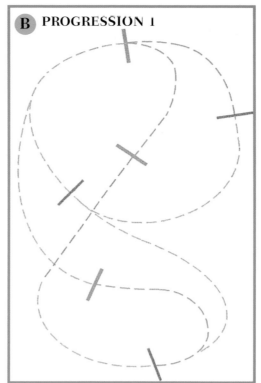

B PROGRESSION 1

Add poles to create more demanding turns. Some examples are shown via the green lines.

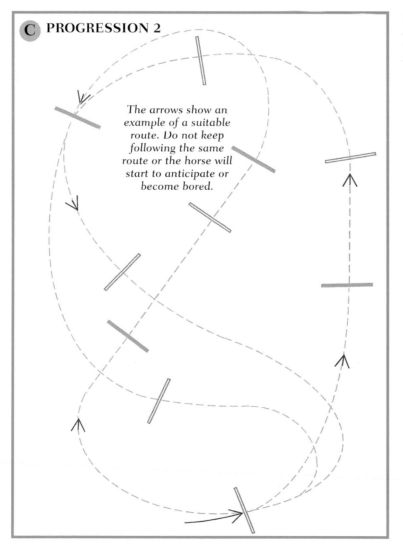

C PROGRESSION 2

The arrows show an example of a suitable route. Do not keep following the same route or the horse will start to anticipate or become bored.

Create unmeasured distances between a few of the poles. The green lines show some examples.

Canter poles in front of and behind a single fence

Uses
- Improves agility, communication, ability to adjust the stride

Unsuitable for
- A horse that is not already used to cantering over poles on the floor

This exercise helps to position the horse at the optimum take-off spot and encourages a good rounded shape (bascule) over the fence. Placing the poles a stride away from the jump is ideal for young horses as it gives them time to sort their legs out while helping them to develop good technique. For the more experienced, the poles can be used to develop a short-striding horse's ability to lengthen and a long-striding horse's ability to shorten. This is also a useful way of correcting problems with flying changes as you can use the last pole to assist the change.

Your horse must be confident over poles on the floor before you use them with a fence; in this respect this exercise is a progression of the previous one (pp. 34–35).

SETTING UP

- Place a cross pole in the centre of your working area. Then place a ground pole a stride in front of the fence and a stride after it. As a rule, the pole on the landing side should be 30cm (1ft) further away from the jump.
- Use heavy poles on the floor so they will not move if the horse clips them.
- In a small area, or with an inexperienced horse, create more room by placing the fence on the long side. You will need to move the poles each time you change the rein.

GETTING STARTED

1 Canter over some individual poles as part of your warm-up. If you are aiming to alter the stride length, do some shortening and lengthening prior to starting the exercise. This is not a suitable exercise for trot.

2 Begin by using a cross pole, to guide the horse to the centre of the fence. It is important to get your line right, so make sure you have enough space to get straight for the first pole and to stay straight for at least one stride after the last one.

PROGRESSING

3 Once you have established balance and rhythm over the cross pole, raise it to a vertical (straight bar).

4 At this stage, you can start to move the poles. Move them a maximum of 30cm (1ft) at a time. If you are unsure of what you are doing, leave them alone!

5 Before you finish, take the poles on the floor away to check that the exercise has had the desired effect. If not, finish on a good jump anyway and then spend time (off the horse) thinking about why. See 'Fixing common faults' on the next page.

SET-UP

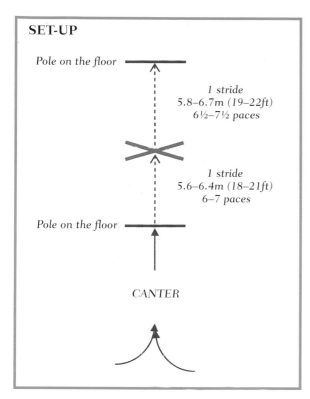

Pole on the floor

1 stride
5.8–6.7m (19–22ft)
6½–7½ paces

1 stride
5.6–6.4m (18–21ft)
6–7 paces

Pole on the floor

CANTER

Place a small fence in the centre of your working area. The horse canters one stride over the pole, one stride before the cross pole, jumps, takes one stride, and then canters over the final pole.

Left: Here the horse is jumping rather flat over the fence and the highest point of the jump is after the fence instead of over the top of it. Compare this sequence with the one below.

How to ride it

- **Ride over the centre** of each pole and the jump.
- **The canter must remain the same** all the way around the arena. Circle to vary the work and help maintain the canter.
- **Decide which way you are going** before you make the first turn, and stick to it. Guide the horse to land on the correct lead by maintaining a degree of turning aids throughout the line, while staying straight.
- **If you land on the wrong lead** and your horse is already doing flying changes, you can change lead over the pole. Otherwise, change through trot, *after* the pole. Make sure you allow room for this. Note that, other than flying changes, transitions should not be made while going over poles.

Fixing common faults

Lack of straightness: Are your turns balanced? If not, you will have to allow more space before the fence and use more circling. Have you set the distance too short, so your horse jinks to the side to allow himself more room? Are you focused on where you are going? If he is worrying about which way he should go at the end, he is likely to meander. No horse can go straight over fences until he goes straight on the flat.

Minimal change to stride length: You need to establish lengthening and shortening on the flat before you can expect to adjust the stride while jumping. It takes time to change habits; reward the horse when he tries.

Tripping over the poles: If you stay forward after the jump, either to pat the horse or due to a lack of balance, he is likely to trip over the last pole. Make certain that you allow the horse to see the poles and have sufficient impulsion (energy). Maintain a constant rhythm and good balance all the way through the exercise and be especially aware of this on the approach to the poles.

Below: In this sequence, the highest part of the jump is over the fence and the horse takes a sensible stride before the pole. That he has jumped the pole shows he is careful, which is great.

Lunge jump

Karen Dixon

Uses

- To regain the horse's natural jump
- For variety and fun
- To save time
- To enable observation

Unsuitable for

- Anyone who is not proficient at lungeing
- Horses that are unused to working on the lunge, or who are not calm and responsive when lunged
- Use in an unenclosed area

Lungeing the horse over a fence helps to maintain his natural jump, free of the weight of the rider. All lungeing can be useful in getting a lazy horse to work without him realizing he is doing so. Jumping on the lunge adds variety, encourages the horse to think for himself, and is fun! It is also a useful timesaver as 10–15 minutes is generally enough. Additionally, any superficial injuries (in the girth or saddle area) can be given time to heal by working the horse in this way. From the ground, you can observe your horse as he jumps and analyse any problems with his style. By looking at his natural way of jumping, you can see how best to ride him, and adapt accordingly. I once had a horse that I tried to ride in a round outline, but watching him lunge jumping I noticed he liked to have his head much higher, with more freedom in his neck. So I started riding him like that; took the martingale off, left his head higher, left the freedom in his neck and he never touched a pole after that. It is up to you to adapt to how your horse wants to jump – they are the athletes, not us; we just sit on them and go.

As with everything to do with horses, preventing problems is much easier than curing them: your horse must be used to being lunged and be responsive to your voice commands before you do this exercise. You must be confident lungeing without jumps before you lunge with them. This exercise is not for you if you tend to get in a mess with the lunge line – horses can become very frightened if you drop the line while they are moving.

SETTING UP

- Position the fence on the long side, near the end of the arena, with enough space for the horse to land and continue on the circle.
- This placement enables maximum control as the horse is slowed by jumping towards the short side. It also allows for circling in front of the fence, ensuring a good line of approach.

GETTING STARTED

1 If your horse has not jumped for a while, or is unfamiliar with poles on the floor, have a jump under saddle first. You have more control when on board, and it is easier for him to jump straight than while on a circle.

2 Start by lungeing over a pole so you can check your line of approach (diagram A). Placing the jump at one end of the working area gives you space to circle in front of the fence, and the end of the arena helps to dissuade horses from speeding off after the jump.

3 Build the jump (see diagram B), starting with a cross pole, which will help guide the horse to the centre of the fence. Start in trot and keep quietly coming back to trot if he canters, but do not interrupt his last three strides of approach or his first stride on landing.

PROGRESSING

4 Wait until the horse is confident over the cross pole, and stays in a quiet rhythm, before progressing further. Gradually increase to a vertical, then to a spread and finally to a parallel (oxer). However, do not push your horse to progress faster than he is ready to; first ensure you have a good balanced jump from a steady, rhythmic canter.

5 This is not a good way to find out how high your horse can jump! If you overface or worry him, he will not forget easily, if at all. The same applies if you keep going too long: constant circling is tiring, so 10–15 minutes once a week is enough.

6 You can add trot or canter poles on the floor, before and after the fence, 2.7–3m (9–10ft) away. This will slow the horse down and encourage him to make the highest point of his jump over the fence and not beyond it. Therefore, if he is diving over the fence, placing a pole the other side will help to correct this (see photograph opposite).

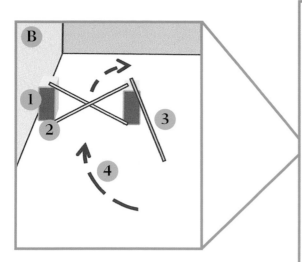

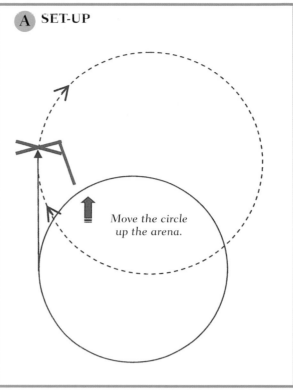

A SET-UP

Move the circle up the arena.

Set up a fence on the long side as shown in diagram B with enough space for the horse to land and continue the circle.

1 *There must be no gap between the wall of the arena and the jump.*

2 *Use blocks rather than jump stands, so there is nothing to catch the lunge line on.*

3 *Lean a pole on to the block to encourage the horse into the fence.*

4 *Jump in the direction shown, then change the rein by moving the sloping pole to the other side of the fence – though this means you cannot circle in front of it. Never have a sloping pole on both sides at once, as it is easy for the lunge line to be caught underneath the one on the landing side.*

Equipment

- Make sure the lunge cavesson fits snugly and does not ride up into the horse's eye on the outside if he leans away from you. It is inadvisable to pass the lunge line through the bit rings of a bridle unless you are very experienced, as you will probably catch the horse in the mouth at some point.

- Wear gloves and NEVER wrap the line around your hand.

- You need a functional lunge whip – an old one, half its original length, is no good!

- Your horse should wear boots all round, but no gadgets – he needs complete freedom of movement.

The pole should be in the middle of the horse's stride. Here it is about a foot too far from the fence so the horse is having to stretch over it.

Technique

- **Take your time.** Circle away from the jump frequently and use this to maintain or regain balance and rhythm. Position yourself slightly behind the horse for the approach, and then move to the landing side while letting out the line (diagram C). Gather the line in again and guide the horse to the inner track if you are missing the fence next time around. All this must happen smoothly.

- **Be constantly aware of the jump** so you do not prompt a refusal by coming into the fence when you intended to miss it out. Watch the horse's eye and his ears. They will tell you if he is happy and thinking forwards, or afraid, resentful or being plain cheeky.

- **The tone of your voice is more important** than the words you say, but you must be consistent.

- **Remember to give the horse a breather** now and again, either by walking or allowing him to go on around a larger circle away from the fence. Changing the rein allows the horse a break while you adjust the fence.

- **Lunge on your own,** or with just one helper, if possible. This avoids distractions and helps the horse to focus.

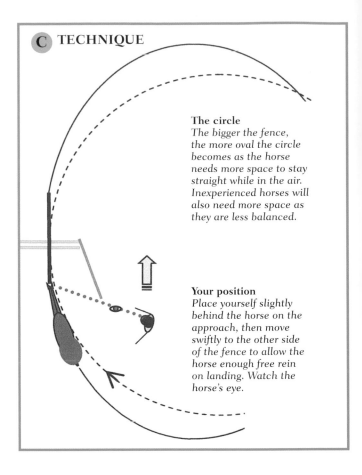

C TECHNIQUE

The circle
The bigger the fence, the more oval the circle becomes as the horse needs more space to stay straight while in the air. Inexperienced horses will also need more space as they are less balanced.

Your position
Place yourself slightly behind the horse on the approach, then move swiftly to the other side of the fence to allow the horse enough free rein on landing. Watch the horse's eye.

- *The great thing about lunge jumping is that you can correct a horse's way of going. For example, if you want to slow him down a bit you can put poles on the floor; if you need to encourage him to be a bit bolder you just build the fence and keep him moving on the circle and over the fence.*

- *I would not balance the pole on the arena fence as in the photo below as the pole could move and cause a problem; it would be much safer to use a wing on the left side of the fence.*

Fixing common faults

Losing rhythm: Circle to re-establish the trot or canter before returning to the exercise.

Refusals: Ask yourself why he stopped. Did you have enough impulsion? A good rhythm is useless without sufficient energy. Make the fence small enough to jump from a standstill. It is off-putting if you are ahead of him (see diagram C). Go back a stage or two to regain his confidence. If he is running rings around you, improve your lungeing before jumping him on the lunge and seek assistance. Always finish on a good note, before your horse becomes bored or tired. If things have gone wrong, do something easy, which you can reward him for, before you stop.

Lack of control: Working nearer to the horse, by shortening the lunge line, gives you more control but means you have to move faster and be quicker to let out and gather in the line. Do not approach the fence if he has lost the rhythm.

Over-exuberance: Let him have a buck and a play and get it out of his system before you start jumping. If you know he is likely to be excitable, pick a day when he is a bit tired, or hack first so you have the best chance of getting him to concentrate. Once he is used to the routine, he should settle.

It is good to see the horse is jumping straight over the middle of the fence; his hind legs are in the trace of his forelegs. Note that the horse has his right ear turned to listen to Antoinette.

■ *Once they are jumping the fence well then you can adapt it, for example by putting a barrel under it.*

■ *Don't take problems head on; if you have a problem with, say, water trays or bullfinches, lunge the horse over them to build his confidence rather than having an uncomfortable jump and risking catching him in the mouth. That also gives the rider confidence as they see the horse jump the obstacle.*

A star of corners

Karen Dixon

Uses

- Introducing complex fences and practising a cross-country fence
- Accuracy, straightness and steering
- Communication and building up the trust between horse and rider

Unsuitable for

- Horses that do not go straight on the flat
- Horses that are not confident over simple angles and arrowheads
- Horses that do not listen to the rider

Corners and arrowheads demand accuracy, straightness and good communication between horse and rider; this exercise includes both types of jump. It also helps to familiarize the horse with fences that give him a bit more to look at, as cross-country fences often look complicated, which can be visually confusing.

Set at its full extent, this is quite advanced because there is a lot for the horse to take in, and you can include tight turns and wider corners. However, it is possible to make it easy to start with and build up gradually.

SETTING UP

- Place a jump block in the centre of the arena at X and build the fence out from it.
- You can use poles on the ground for route 1, shown in diagram A, but not for the routes in diagrams B, C and D.

GETTING STARTED

1 Start your training session with arrowheads if you have not done any recently.

2 Warm up in trot and canter over the arms of the fence (route 1, diagram A).

3 To start the exercise, ride through the central route (2) in trot. You can walk over the block if you have a problem, but do not turn away or allow the horse over one of the arms of the jump. This part of the exercise helps to develop the straightness required to jump the corners. You are also making sure that the horse is confident with the poles angled in this manner.

4 Narrow the angle of the arms for route 2 (diagram A).

PROGRESSING

4 Jump the corners, starting with a narrow angle so you can jump the centre of each pole, as shown (diagram B). Again, trot will give you more control. (Refer to diagram A on p. 91 for how to approach a corner.)

5 Increase the angle of the corners. As you do so, move your line of approach closer to the central block.

6 Once you are successfully cantering over the corners, add the E–B route in again (see diagram C).

7 Put a course together. Plan your route before you start (diagram D). The general rule is to begin with a straightforward jump and build towards something more difficult. The two routes shown in diagram D are just two examples of that rule in practice.

8 This is quite an intense exercise because of the more collected canter needed to jump precisely and to navigate tight turns. Go large and lengthen the canter occasionally to give the horse a break and keep the canter energized. Before you finish, it is nice to let the horse jump a straightforward spread fence that he can move on into – for fun!

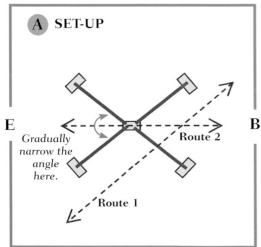

A SET-UP

E — Route 2 — B

Gradually narrow the angle here.

Route 1

Place a jump block in the centre of the arena at X and build the fence as shown. Warm up by jumping the arms, then jump through the centre.

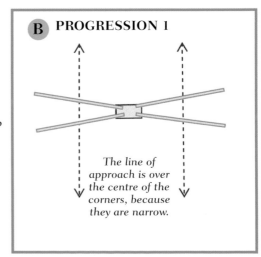

B PROGRESSION 1

The line of approach is over the centre of the corners, because they are narrow.

Narrow the arms and start jumping the corners, gradually increasing the angle of them.

Play around jumping the sides of the jump before you take on the middle element.

The horse has met the fence in the middle; he is concentrating and is completely focused. Because of all the poles, the horse has to have a connection with the rider in order to trust him and make the jump. This type of small fence builds the relationship between horse and rider.

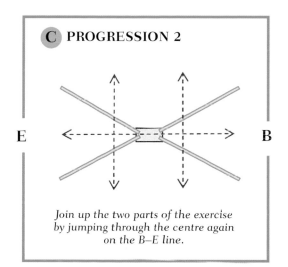

C PROGRESSION 2

E ← → B

Join up the two parts of the exercise by jumping through the centre again on the B–E line.

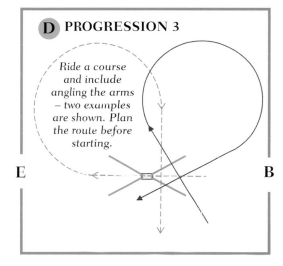

D PROGRESSION 3

Ride a course and include angling the arms – two examples are shown. Plan the route before starting.

E B

How to ride it

- **Be precise.** This is just as important with a very small fence as with a big one. If you let your horse meander into small fences in a disrespectful manner, he is unlikely to listen to you ahead of a bigger fence. Nor will he understand why you are suddenly giving him different instructions. If you are on the wrong line, not straight, or have lost the quality of the pace (balance, rhythm and impulsion), circle away from the fence.

- **Sit still.** It is difficult for the horse to stay straight unless you are sitting quietly.

- **Stare at the part of the fence you want to jump** and make sure that you jump that spot.

- **Maintain an even pressure with the reins** and keep the leg on so you do not get in front of the movement. Keep your hands low and wide, and ride with both legs equally.

- **Approaching a corner or an arrowhead on a long stride is not an option.** If you have seen a long one, just keep waiting for the fence and hold your line. Give the horse the chance to pop a short stride in before the fence if he wants to. Going for a long one will not help the horse's confidence and is likely to result in a run-out.

Fixing common faults

Panicking: Some horses (and riders!) get very worried by anything different. Going over blocks on the floor and poles at angles to one another can make them nervous. Go back a step or two and reward progress, however small. Get to know your horse so you are always a step ahead of him.

Lack of straightness: Any problems with straightness should be apparent during the first parts of the exercise. If the horse is confused about route 2 in diagram A, walk through it. Do not make the exercise any more difficult until such problems are resolved. If the horse is not going forwards, he will be very difficult to keep straight. Make sure you are riding from the leg and go large to regain forward movement. It is tempting to use too much hand when you are aiming for an exact spot; this distracts him and stops him going forwards. Is the lack of straightness due to your turns? If so, look round earlier and get into the habit of keeping your eye on the fence during the turn.

Losing balance on the turns: Check the quality of the pace and improve it, if necessary, using circles and transitions.

Virginia Elliot MBE

Ginny Elliot is one of the most successful event riders of all time. She holds two Olympic team silver and two individual bronze medals, as well as two World Championship titles. She has won Badminton three times, on three different horses, and Burghley five times. Her European Championship record is equally impressive with four team, and three individual gold medals.

Ginny has long been renowned for producing top-class eventers, and is now successfully training point-to-pointers. She has been a patron of Spinal Research since 2002.

More... www.ginnyelliot.com

Favourite achievements

★ *1986 was a fantastic year for me. I won the World Championships in Australia and the team won gold as well, so that was a real bonus. Then I won the alternative World Championships in Poland at Bialy Bor – and I won Burghley that year too. That meant I had done a Grand Slam of three four-stars in a year, which was a really big achievement and a big highlight for me – a sort of pipedream. Sadly there was no prize for that back then!*

★ *Being lucky enough to compete at two Olympics (Los Angeles and Seoul) was a fantastic thrill. And I very much enjoyed going back to help in Atlanta as a team co-ordinator/trainer – it was really nice to go to the Olympics again with a different job.*

Ginny Elliot on Priceless at the Los Angeles Olympics.

TRAINING PHILOSOPHY

■ To train a three-day event horse successfully, all aspects of his care and training must be taken into account and given equal priority. If he is in a happy and calm environment, he is much more likely to make good progress. There are no short cuts; training is a slow process that must be tailored to each individual horse and allowed to proceed in a natural way. Throughout, it is important to keep listening to your horse and making adjustments accordingly.

■ At Hollier's, we firmly adhere to the principle that prevention is better than cure. We avoid setbacks like the plague because they take so long to resolve and may leave lasting damage. However, when a problem does arise, it is far better to do a little every day to resolve it rather than 'grind on' until the horse becomes resentful and unco-operative.

■ Dressage is the cornerstone of training the event horse, as the quality of his flatwork determines the quality of his jumping. If the horse is not straight on the flat, it is impossible for him to be straight over a fence. Riding is also highly influential in the success of your training, since mistakes usually stem from the rider. Work towards making your aids independent of one another and think of your weight (rather than your seat) as an aid. While an element of luck is involved, correct training can prevent problems by allowing the horse time to adjust to the weight of a rider, so that his physical development keeps pace with his work.

■ Training is a constant learning process and you must adapt your methods to suit each horse, but it is tremendously rewarding when it is successful.

ADVICE TO NEWCOMERS

A horse already knows it is a horse; the art of horsemanship lies solely with the rider. I have always tried to remember that, because it covers all aspects of training. The horse actually knows how to do everything; it is a question of asking him to do what you want, when you wish to do it.

Introduction to the exercises

Grids are suitable for most horses and riders, and they form an essential part of any training programme. Those on the following pages provide a starting point; vary them to keep the horse interested. All the grids help to build confidence, straightness and gymnastic ability. However, jumping grids that are beyond your horse's current stage of training and fitness may cause injury in the long term. Grids are hard work for the horse, so a 20-minute session once a week is generally enough.

Uses

- Agility and straightness

- Maintenance of the horse's natural bascule

- Rider's jumping technique

- Rider and horse confidence

Unsuitable for

- Horses unable to go forwards and straight – grids help develop straightness but do not create it

- Horses or riders unable to jump a single small fence confidently in reasonable balance

Grids help the horse to develop athletically and become quick on his feet (to 'pat the ground', as opposed to thumping it). They are not only an essential part of training a young horse, but are also invaluable throughout his career. They help to develop confidence and straightness, and improve the quality of the horse's natural bascule (roundness over the fence). They also improve the rider's confidence, general jumping technique and position.

SETTING UP

- Place the fences off the track at the side of the arena at first.
- Put up one or more individual fences, with or without placing poles. Build two cross rails (cross poles) one stride apart (diagram A).
- Correct jumping distances between the fences of a grid are vital, especially for inexperienced horses or riders. The distances may be lengthened by 30cm (1ft) or so, but it is rare that you will need to need to shorten them.
- Do not be tempted to start with four fences as it is very daunting for a horse to be suddenly faced with a mass of poles.

GETTING STARTED

1 To warm up, jump one or more individual fences from trot, with or without placing poles.

2 Start with the two cross rails (diagram A). If your horse has not jumped a grid before, make the fences small enough to jump from a standstill.

3 When he is jumping confidently, add the next two cross rails, one at a time.

PROGRESSING

4 Listen to your horse. Is he enjoying the work? When to progress depends on the horse's temperament, balance and capacity to learn. Two sessions of the same thing is too much repetition. There are no short cuts. Our motto at Hollier's is 'If in doubt, don't'. This applies to all aspects of training.

5 Change the cross poles to verticals (diagram B), but only when the horse remains straight all the way through the grid. Short-coupled horses tend to find it easier to stay straight than long-striding ones because the latter type will be tempted to allow themselves extra space by angling left or right.

6 The next step is to add an oxer (spread), then a final vertical (diagram C). The oxer encourages roundness and the horse is discouraged from jumping too extravagantly over it by the final vertical.

> ### How to ride it
> - **Make sure the horse is straight** before you reach the first element.
> - **Keep your own weight central.** Do not lean left or right over the jumps. Focus on where you are going.
> - **Give the horse enough rein** to stretch over the jumps.
> - **Do not interfere** until the horse has taken one stride away from the last element.

A placing pole 2.7m (9ft) in front of the first jump ensures that the horse arrives at the perfect take-off spot. However, horse and rider should not be allowed to become reliant on such extra assistance.

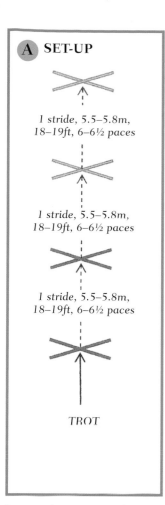

A SET-UP

1 stride, 5.5–5.8m,
18–19ft, 6–6½ paces

1 stride, 5.5–5.8m,
18–19ft, 6–6½ paces

1 stride, 5.5–5.8m,
18–19ft, 6–6½ paces

TROT

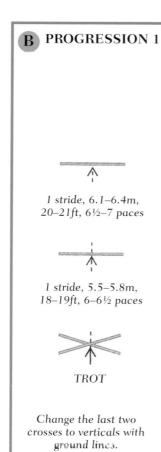

B PROGRESSION 1

1 stride, 6.1–6.4m,
20–21ft, 6½–7 paces

1 stride, 5.5–5.8m,
18–19ft, 6–6½ paces

TROT

*Change the last two
crosses to verticals with
ground lines.*

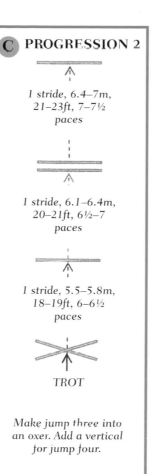

C PROGRESSION 2

1 stride, 6.4–7m,
21–23ft, 7–7½
paces

1 stride, 6.1–6.4m,
20–21ft, 6½–7
paces

1 stride, 5.5–5.8m,
18–19ft, 6–6½
paces

TROT

*Make jump three into
an oxer. Add a vertical
for jump four.*

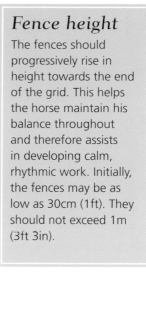

Fence height

The fences should progressively rise in height towards the end of the grid. This helps the horse maintain his balance throughout and therefore assists in developing calm, rhythmic work. Initially, the fences may be as low as 30cm (1ft). They should not exceed 1m (3ft 3in).

Virginia Elliot

*Begin with two cross poles a
stride apart, then add a third
and fourth.*

Fixing common faults

Prevention is better than cure. When you encounter a problem, ask yourself what you could have done to prevent it. Resorting to abusive methods is a sure sign you have failed to listen to your horse.

Refusals: Make the fences small enough to jump from a standstill. Turning away from a fence is the fastest way to teach your horse to refuse. Setting incorrect distances or over-jumping the same grid can also result in refusals. Another reason for refusals in a grid is over-facing your horse by adding too many fences too soon, or raising them too much.

Rushing: The horse must feel confident he will have the full use of his head and neck or he may start to rush out of fear. If he is simply over-exuberant, release some of the energy first (hack first, school second for example). Try to work with your horse, not against him. Go back a stage to trotting poles in front of a small cross rail 2.7m (9ft) away to re-establish concentration and a calm rhythm. Never ask your horse to do anything you are not confident doing.

Lack of straightness through the grid: Your approach must be straight with your horse maintaining rhythm round the turn and going forwards. Your weight must remain central. If the horse speeds up through the grid he may lose straightness to give himself more space. Check your turn, the rhythm, the distances and your own focus. Stick with cross poles until you have resolved the problem. If you cannot ride straight down the quarter line without fences, you will not be able to with them.

Keeping your horse interested

■ **Never grind on with the same thing** so your horse becomes bored and resentful – one or two 20-minute jumping sessions a week is plenty for a youngster. Older horses also need variety.

■ **Vary the position of the grid** to keep your horse on his toes. Move the fences to the other side of the arena, the quarter or centre line. Notice how your horse reacts – going towards or away from home, for example. It is not very beneficial to place the grid on the diagonal, however, due to the increased risk of a poor turn.

■ **Change the distances** (one, two or three strides between fences).

Introducing bounces

Uses

■ Agility and straightness

■ Maintenance of natural bascule

■ Rider's jumping technique

■ Rider and horse confidence

Unsuitable for

■ Horses with joint or stiffness problems

■ Riders who are unable to move quickly and smoothly to stay in balance

This exercise is used to sharpen the horse's technique, improve his athleticism and encourage elasticity. It demands rhythm and a constant pace and will help to improve the horse's canter. The rider must develop balance independent of the horse to allow him to get on with the job.

Bounces are a natural progression of the 'Introducing grids' exercise, and that exercise applies equally here. They can be introduced as soon as horse and rider are confident over two fences a stride apart.

SETTING UP

■ Start with one or more individual fences, with or without placing poles. Then build two cross rails (cross poles) one stride apart before creating a bounce.

■ The bounce must be small enough to jump from a standstill.

■ Use cross poles to begin with to discourage the horse from wandering left or right.

GETTING STARTED

1 Warm up as for the previous exercise, then ride some fences a stride apart.

2 If you or your horse have not jumped a bounce before, start as shown in diagram A. Be aware that the horse may drop behind your leg after he has finished the exercise, falling into trot.

3 The more experienced can start as shown in diagram B. The vertical before the bounce helps the horse arrive in the perfect place for take-off and the single canter stride ensures he is going forwards and straight.

4 It is paramount that the horse remains straight throughout the grid. If you are not sure that this is happening ask someone to observe you by looking down the grid as you are jumping. If you are tilting your body to the left or right, you can cause a lack of straightness in your horse. Make sure you keep your balance over his centre of gravity.

PROGRESSING

5 Once you are able to maintain calmness, rhythm and straightness through the grid and after it, raise the fences by a hole or two.

6 Then add a second bounce to a square oxer (parallel). Build the oxer gradually: start with a vertical, then make it into a spread before squaring it. This last element is a test of the quality of the horse's bascule. You should have a wonderful feeling of his rounding over that element in particular.

How to ride it

■ **Ride straight before and after the jumps.**

■ **Keep your eye concentrating entirely on the fence.** There should be nothing you need to do in preparation for a fence that causes you to take your eye off it. You should not need to look down to check the length of your reins or to see which leg the horse is leading on; learn to assess these things by feel. Nor should it be necessary to look down in order to switch your stick to the other hand or to shorten your reins. As you approach the grid look at the top pole of the first fence. If you get the approach to the first fence correct, the rest should follow.

■ **Keep your upper body still** as you go through the grid, with a light, slightly forward seat. The small of your back should feel slightly concave – this keeps you from collapsing (this works on the flat as well!).

■ **Achieve a constant contact with your hands** by thinking about controlling the reins through the elbows – trust me it works – this will encourage your elbows to be elastic and your wrists to relax, allowing the horse to move forwards through the jumps in an unrestricted fashion.

■ **Move fluidly with the horse and avoid taking off before him.** Folding too early places your weight on the horse's forelegs just as he is attempting to lift them off the ground.

Fixing common faults

All faults relating to the previous exercise apply to this one.

Below: At this point she is looking good.

The difference between a bounce and a normal landing stride

Below: Between bounces: the horse is already preparing to take off again before he has finished landing over the last jump. He is more tense in his hindquarters than in the other photo, and the line from his neck to his forefoot is more vertical. He has raised his head and neck and is about to put both hind feet down at once to take off. Therefore, he is moving his weight back, off his forehand – which is why it is so important for the rider to sit up between bounces.

Above: The first stride after the grid. With no other fences to jump, the horse's centre of gravity is further forwards than in the other photo.

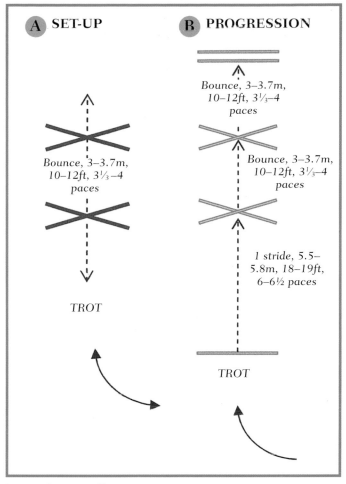

Bounce, 3–3.7m, 10–12ft, 3⅓–4 paces

Bounce, 3–3.7m, 10–12ft, 3⅓–4 paces

Bounce, 3–3.7m, 10–12ft, 3⅓–4 paces

1 stride, 5.5–5.8m, 18–19ft, 6–6½ paces

TROT

TROT

Start with two small cross poles. Approach in trot from either direction, then canter away.

Start with three cross rails then change the first to a vertical. Finally, add an oxer.

Below: Here the rider is in front of the movement, which is potentially a rather dangerous route. It is at this moment – on take off – that riders are most likely to get in front of the horse.

Below: Again, this is very good with the upper body. The hands could be lower though, and there should be more weight through the heel of the lower leg.

Below: This is a great improvement on the picture above, but if the rider's seat had been lower in the saddle, bringing her shoulders slightly higher, that would have been the perfect scenario.

Below: This is very good: good freedom of head and neck with the hands, the lower leg is excellent and the upper body is very good.

Grids for novices

Uses

- Agility, straightness and maintenance of natural bascule

- Rider's jumping technique and rider and horse confidence

Unsuitable for

- Horses that are unable to go forwards and straight

- Horses or riders that are unused to more simple grids or not yet confident over bounces

These grids are suitable for Intro, Pre-Novice and Novice-level eventers. By the time a horse is competing at Novice level he may have begun to develop some imperfections in his style, such as flattening over the fences, due to increasing his speed cross-country. Grids can help to correct these problems. They are particularly useful for long-striding horses at any level as they encourage the horse to shorten his stride and improve the quality of his bascule.

These grids are a natural progression of the previous ones (p. 46 and 48), and their text applies equally here.

SETTING UP

- Place two cross rails (cross poles) a stride apart on the centre or quarter line.
- The actual distances for all the grids will depend on the height of the fences as well as the horse's conformation, age, experience and length of stride, so you should not rely too much on the tape measure.

GETTING STARTED

1 Build the grid gradually until it is set as shown in diagram A. Change the cross rails to verticals only when the horse remains straight.

PROGRESSING

2 Continue as shown in diagrams B and C.

3 Vary the distances between the fences by 30cm (1ft) or so to encourage shortening or lengthening.

4 Once the horse has completed a few novice events, vary the fence height through the grid rather than progressively increasing it. For example, 84cm (2ft 9in) first fence, 90cm (3ft) second fence, 84cm (2ft 9in) third fence. This teaches him to cope with the unexpected and remain in balance.

5 All exercise builds muscle, but jumping muscles only increase through actually jumping. They will build up gradually through each jumping session but this is a slow process. It can be misleading, because the horse may look well developed but still lack the strength to manage difficult fences or demanding grids.

6 I never make the lesson the same two weeks running; I have a better chance of keeping the horse's interest if he is not aware of what is coming next! I play it by ear, taking into account his temperament and individual ability.

7 The week after concentrating on gridwork, I might do one quick grid to a round of fences. You need no more than four jumps – an oxer, a vertical and two together to form a double – to have a short course. The two single fences can be jumped from both directions and possibly the double as well, depending on how it is built.

How to ride it

- **Focus your attention** on the top of the first fence from at least six strides away. This will help you to develop an eye for a stride. Do not look for a stride, look for a stride pattern, which is not the same thing. At oxers, always focus on the centre of the front, top rail.

- **Pay attention to how the horse feels** at every stage throughout the grid and develop a habit of interrogating yourself about it.

Fixing common faults

All faults relating to the previous exercise also apply to this one. You can help overcome most problems by building fences up within a grid. If the distance between them is correct, the horse will meet each at the right spot and gain tremendous confidence as a result.

Flattening: The bascule can be improved by slightly shortening the distance between the fences, thereby requiring the horse to land sooner and round more.

Lack of straightness: Use poles on the ground at right angles to the fences to act as tram lines and assist in keeping the horse straight. Start with these at the full fence width, then gradually move them in. For an Advanced eventer they could end up as little as 90cm (3ft) apart.

A SET-UP

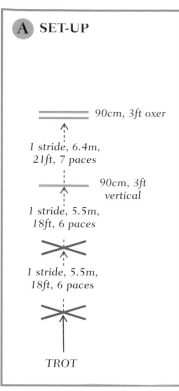

———— 90cm, 3ft oxer
↑
1 stride, 6.4m,
21ft, 7 paces

——— 90cm, 3ft
vertical
↑
1 stride, 5.5m,
18ft, 6 paces

✕
↑
1 stride, 5.5m,
18ft, 6 paces

✕
↑
TROT

Begin with two cross rails to
encourage straightness. Novice
horses should always approach in
trot; Intermediate eventers could
approach in canter.

B PROGRESSION 1

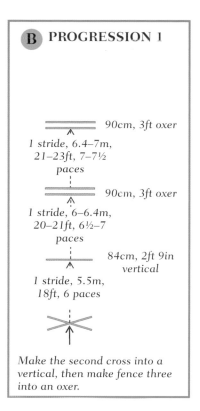

———— 90cm, 3ft oxer
↑
1 stride, 6.4–7m,
21–23ft, 7–7½
paces

———— 90cm, 3ft oxer
↑
1 stride, 6–6.4m,
20–21ft, 6½–7
paces

——— 84cm, 2ft 9in
vertical
↑
1 stride, 5.5m,
18ft, 6 paces

✕
↑

Make the second cross into a
vertical, then make fence three
into an oxer.

C PROGRESSION 2

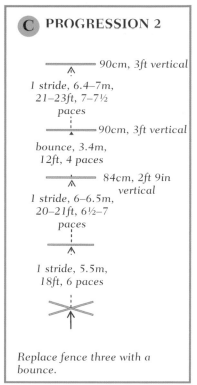

———— 90cm, 3ft vertical
↑
1 stride, 6.4–7m,
21–23ft, 7–7½
paces

——— 90cm, 3ft vertical
↓
bounce, 3.4m,
12ft, 4 paces

——— 84cm, 2ft 9in
vertical
↑
1 stride, 6–6.5m,
20–21ft, 6½–7
paces

✕
↑
1 stride, 5.5m,
18ft, 6 paces

✕
↑

Replace fence three with a
bounce.

Distances

While it may be feasible to lengthen the distances between these fences by as much as 30cm (1ft), it is rare to shorten them. The shorter the distance, the more effort will be required for the horse to collect himself in time for the next jump.

How often?

Schooling a young or novice horse over jumps need not happen any more often than once a week, unless you are experiencing particular problems. I would not require horses that are good at jumping to go over grids and a course of single fences on the same day. They will do one or the other for about 10 minutes, which is quite enough.

A good bascule, below, in comparison to a flatter jump, right. The arc is very good from nose to tail and shows a true bascule through the shoulders and just behind the saddle. However, the rider's lower leg isn't good and she has slightly chucked her upper body forwards. Also, I would have had the hands a bit lower rather than along the neck. If the lower leg had been correct the whole picture would look quite nice. This shot is repeated from p. 21 for comparison purposes.

This horse hasn't got the same bascule over the fence, therefore it looks a flatter jump. Looking at the line along the top of the horse, from the ears to the tail: ideally the head should be lower than it is, and the shoulders a little higher. One would be trying to work the horse through gymnastics to get it to lower its head more and bring its shoulders up higher. The position of the rider is very good.

Photo by Sheila Fitzsimons.

Grids for the advanced horse

Virginia Elliot

Uses
- Agility and straightness
- Maintenance of natural bascule
- Correcting faults in jumping technique

Unsuitable for
- Novice horses
- Horses with joint or stiffness problems

These exercises are intended for Advanced eventers. However, the difficulties encountered in each grid should be no more testing than those the horse met at Novice level, when he was less experienced. Even for an advanced horse, grids continue to improve both horse and rider's jumping technique. They help to correct any imperfections before these become real problems or bad habits. Varying the distances and fence heights will teach the horse to adapt and keep thinking for himself. He has to learn to get in close to spread fences and to back off at verticals, ensuring that the highest part of the bascule is always over the middle of the fence (viewed from the side). Grids can help to achieve this.

SETTING UP

- Start with placing pole to a cross pole (diagram A).
- The first fence will normally be slightly lower than the next, even if the heights then vary through the grid.
- Use the distances shown on the diagrams as a starting point.

GETTING STARTED

1 Begin with the grid in diagram A, building it up gradually. This is more difficult than the Novice level grids (pp.50–51) because it requires more effort to bounce over an oxer than a vertical.

PROGRESSING

2 At this level, the fence heights and distances can be varied more than for the Novice horse. The grid can also be used as part of a course. This will help keep the horse on his toes and interested.

3 By this stage, you should be aware of habitual faults, such as flattening or getting too close, and your grids should be tailored to correct these problems. Every rider needs instruction throughout their career, and an eye on the ground is invaluable in identifying faults early on.

4 Grid C is particularly testing when the oxers are squared as the horse must jump each correctly in order to meet the next fence at the correct take-off point.

Fixing common faults

Too close to verticals: If the horse 'props' over verticals by taking off too late, the highest part of the bascule will be after the fence. To help correct this, place a pole on the ground, 60cm (2ft) in front of the fence. Alternatively, add a small fence 15cm (6in) in front.

Flattening over the fence: Priceless preferred to take off 60cm (2ft) early and jump flat. Simply shortening the distances was ineffective as he had no problem shortening his stride. The solution was to use a placing pole 3m (10ft) after the first element of a double, forcing him to land sooner and therefore to round his back more.

Refusals: These can and do happen, even if you have done everything in your power to prevent them! When they do occur, try to be constructive and learn from the mistake. Being critical of yourself and honest about your mistakes can be demoralizing but is ultimately the only way to succeed. If the stop really was not your fault then you must find out what the problem was.

We can see the horse has propped in this stride and moved clearly to the right. The rider has done a good job of not going in front of the movement and still has the intention of jumping the fence. She is keeping a nice open hand right and left to steer the horse straight and has the lower leg engaged to ask the horse to keep going forwards. The horse went on to jump the fence.

How to ride it
- **Fine-tune your ability to listen to your horse** so that you use and adapt the grids appropriately according to your horse's individual needs.
- **Keep developing your eye for a stride.**

A SET-UP

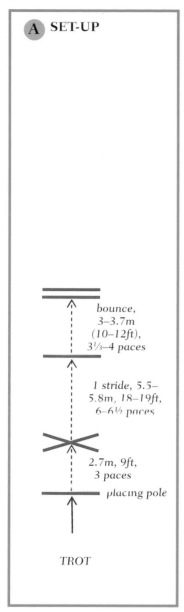

bounce,
3–3.7m
(10–12ft),
3⅓–4 paces

1 stride, 5.5–
5.8m, 18–19ft,
6–6½ paces

2.7m, 9ft,
3 paces

placing pole

TROT

Start with a placing pole to a cross pole and build the grid up gradually.

B PROGRESSION 1

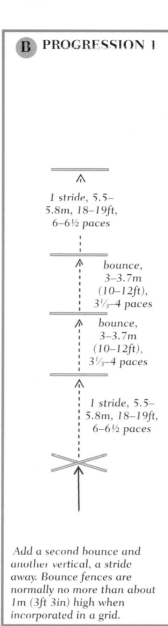

1 stride, 5.5–
5.8m, 18–19ft,
6–6½ paces

bounce,
3–3.7m
(10–12ft),
3⅓–4 paces

bounce,
3–3.7m
(10–12ft),
3⅓–4 paces

1 stride, 5.5–
5.8m, 18–19ft,
6–6½ paces

Add a second bounce and another vertical, a stride away. Bounce fences are normally no more than about 1m (3ft 3in) high when incorporated in a grid.

C PROGRESSION 2

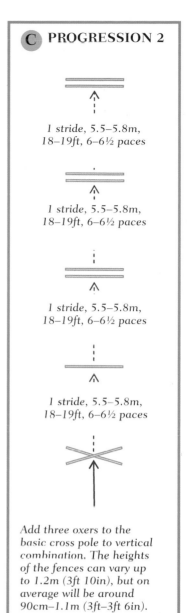

1 stride, 5.5–5.8m,
18–19ft, 6–6½ paces

1 stride, 5.5–5.8m,
18–19ft, 6–6½ paces

1 stride, 5.5–5.8m,
18–19ft, 6–6½ paces

1 stride, 5.5–5.8m,
18–19ft, 6–6½ paces

1 stride, 5.5–5.8m,
18–19ft, 6–6½ paces

Add three oxers to the basic cross pole to vertical combination. The heights of the fences can vary up to 1.2m (3ft 10in), but on average will be around 90cm–1.1m (3ft–3ft 6in).

The horse has taken off at the correct distance from the fence but the forearm is very, very straight, which is not correct technique. The knee should be much higher.

Here, a pole has been placed on the ground out from the fence. Now the horse has brought his forearm up and his knee is in front of him as opposed to the straighter look. This is an improvement. Placing a pole out like this can also teach the horse not to go 'beyond his distance' on the take-off stride: sometimes young horses will take a slightly longer last stride and get a little too deep, even though the stride pattern was good (this also causes them to dangle their front legs). The pole corrects this.

William Fox-Pitt

Favourite achievements

★*Winning the individual silver medal at the 1987 Junior European Championships in Rome. It was my first major success and more of a surprise than anything else. I had a very good, consistent horse but he was much more of a team horse than an individual prospect, so to get a silver medal was a great thrill.*

★*Winning Burghley in 1994; to win your first four-star is realizing a dream. I did it relatively early in my career – it makes you hungrier and is a boost to your confidence. It's also a relief in that if it never happens again, at least you've won a four-star!*

ADVICE TO NEWCOMERS

■ Be fully prepared. Go for it and have fun!

William Fox-Pitt on Tamarillo at the Athens Olympics.

William gained team silver in Athens, his second Olympics. He has successfully represented Britain for over 20 years in international competition, winning team bronze at the World Equestrian Games in Jerez and five European team golds. He has won Burghley (three times) and Badminton and has had numerous placings at both events. He has held the title of Leading UK Rider five times, and topped the FEI world rankings once and been ranked second three times. William is highly regarded within the sport and his board directorship of British Eventing and the Professional Event Riders Association reflects this.

More... www.foxpitteventing.co.uk

TRAINING PHILOSOPHY

■ My main principle of training a horse is to take time. It can take one misjudgment to completely lose a horse's confidence. It is built up in bricks and layers and if the foundations are not there then the end result might not be as solid as I would like.

■ For competing, I have a system and a time-scale in my mind that I work to, but every horse is different and the rate and stage at which they mature varies. Normally, they would not start to compete until the end of their fifth year, and even then they would do only a few events. I would then spend the sixth year doing some Novices and, hopefully, a few Intermediates if things are going well, before aiming at a first two-star three-day event at the end of the seventh year. It is important to take time when horses are both physically and mentally immature. I would rather enjoy riding a 16-year-old horse round Badminton, when he is more of an expert at what he does, than an 8-year-old. As a general rule, what you use up early on in their career, you do not have at the end of it, unless you are exceptionally lucky.

■ I introduce jumping exercises to the horses at a young age to teach them to be athletic, to think for themselves and to keep them interested. Jumping big fences time and time again is no good with event horses. It is much more important to teach them to be handy and supple.

■ One of my main beliefs is that it is vital that a horse enjoys his work. The way to maintain that enjoyment is not to pressurize him into doing anything he is not ready to do and to keep him in a very varied work programme.

■ When I teach other riders I often find they need help to be positive about their riding so that they can give their horse confidence for both dressage and jumping. A lot of riders lack confidence and tend to imagine the worst rather than getting on and riding positively. My book *Schooling for Success* gives further examples and more detail of my training philosophy.

Introduction to the exercises

There is a lot you can teach your horse at home about some of the challenges he will meet cross-country. It is important that he is confident with cross-country concepts, such as jumping at angles and over water trays, before you actually meet these things out in the open. In the more controlled environment of an arena or field you can alter the fences to help the horse if things go wrong.

Mock coffin and trakehner

William Fox-Pitt

Uses

■ To practise a cross-country fence, add variety and hone instinctive reactions

■ To improve and test communication and trust

■ To practise changes of pace

Unsuitable for

■ A horse or rider not yet confident over straightforward fences

It is important to practise cross-country fences in a safe environment; introducing the horse to unfamiliar and potentially spooky obstacles in this way helps to build trust and communication with the rider. These are skills that will be needed at every single event. A spooky fence can be used within many other exercises to test whether you have as much control as you think you do and to add an element of surprise to keep the horse attentive and interested. These fences can also be used to test changes of pace within a course: an upright a few strides after a trakehner or a spread a few strides before a coffin both require a gear change. Any unusual fence will help to improve the instinctive reactions of horse and rider. The ability to ride a coffin well is something all riders should strive to achieve.

Before you introduce anything unusual, the horse must be confident over straightforward fences. Out hacking, go through puddles, over little drainage ditches, past colourful road signs and get him used to seeing as much as possible as part of his everyday routine, preferably with a sensible companion to inspire confidence. The same applies to the rider! The rider must be confident over simple fences and in handling minor difficulties.

SETTING UP

■ Build some fences that the horse will find easy and inviting. Place the water tray near to them but with a clear line for the approach and landing.

■ It is best to use as robust a water tray as possible. Tip any water out of it before you start.

■ Use a ground pole on each side of a plastic tray to encourage the horse to jump it (diagram A). Alternatively, a rubber tray can be used on its own and will bear up to being stood upon.

GETTING STARTED

1 Warm up, and then jump some easy fences so that the horse is confident and attentive before you introduce the new task. Do not make a big issue of new obstacles; incorporate them in other work rather than placing them alone in the centre of the arena (refer to 'Building trust', p. 63).

2 Walk or trot over the tray, making sure you allow the horse to see it. Walk gives you maximum control and promotes calmness; trot keeps the horse thinking forwards. You have far less control in canter so stay in trot until the horse is confident. Jumping back towards the yard at first can give the horse added

incentive to keep going forwards. It does not matter if he takes a big leap over the tray, just keep the leg on and sit still. It is important that you do not catch him in the mouth when he has just decided to be brave – use a breastplate or neck strap to grab hold of if necessary. You are working towards cantering over the water tray, as you would any spread fence.

PROGRESSING

3 The next stage is to put a small fence after the water tray, a stride or so away.

4 Once the horse is happy with that, add a small upright, a stride in front of the tray. You are aiming to maintain rhythm and balance throughout.

5 Another variation is to create a trakehner by placing a pole above the tray. This is jumped as though the tray is not there. Again, approach it in trot until the horse is relaxed about it.

6 Use your imagination and practise spooky fences by draping things on them, or tying bits of plastic to them. Whatever you use must not hurt or frighten the horse if he treads on it or catches it with his hooves. Move the fences to different places in the manège and add them into other exercises so they become routine.

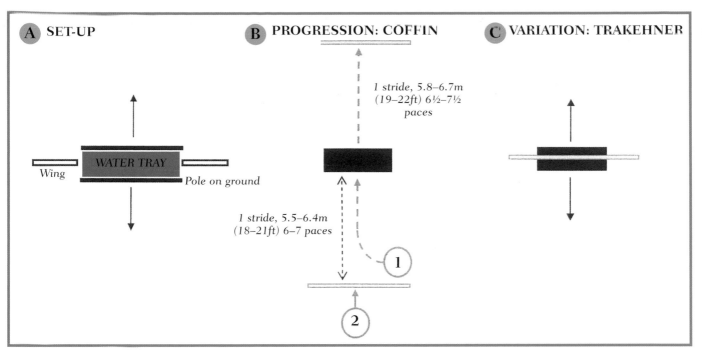

A SET-UP

WATER TRAY

Wing

Pole on ground

1 stride, 5.5–6.4m
(18–21ft) 6–7 paces

B PROGRESSION: COFFIN

1 stride, 5.8–6.7m
(19–22ft) 6½–7½
paces

1

2

C VARIATION: TRAKEHNER

Warm up over some easier fences, then walk or trot back and forth over the water tray. Use a ground pole on each side of a plastic tray. A rubber tray can be used on its own.
1 Walk or trot over the water tray and trot over an upright after it.
2 Trot over all three elements.

In this variation, a pole is placed over the water tray to make a trakehner. Set the pole low enough to jump from a standstill at first.

How to ride it

■ **Be consistent** – approach a small mock coffin the same way you approach the real thing. You need a fairly powerful collected canter – enough power for all three elements and enough collection for an upright followed by something that may cause the horse to want to stop suddenly.

■ **If you visualize having a problem you surely will!** Look up and sit up – the difference that simple act makes to the horse's balance is quite phenomenal. Have the feeling of three-quarters of the horse in front of you, keep the contact and keep your leg around the horse. This helps him feel secure.

Fixing common faults

Refusals: Do not make a big deal out of a stop at something spooky or different. Make it as easy as possible and keep everything low key and quiet. Do not turn away – back up if need be, and then jump from a walk.

Jumping extravagantly: This is often a sign of fear. Jump the fence a few times, back and forth, then return to it regularly as part of other work.

Over-reacting: If the horse is spooking, you need to occupy his mind with something else and apply a degree of quiet but firm discipline. Make the obstacle as inviting and small as possible and work on getting his full attention on work – of any sort. If you over-react, your horse is likely to follow your lead!

This shows how a horse can be spooked by a ditch; it is something that he needs to become confident about. In the far left picture the horse is looking down and while the rider is allowing him to do that, she is maintaining the contact and therefore his confidence. She is keeping her leg on to encourage him forwards. At this stage, we are approaching in trot so that the horse **does** look. He is learning what he is doing and it is easier to correct him and to keep him straight from trot if he decides to run out.

In the next picture (centre left) he is still having a look but is jumping over, which shows that he has confidence in the rider. You would like to think that next time round he might jump the fence more smoothly.

A double of angles

Uses

- Improves communication, accuracy and straightness

Unsuitable for

- Horses that have not jumped individual angled fences or that do not go straight on the flat

This exercise puts angles together in the form of a double. This combination of angles is frequently seen in competition, for example as an alternative to jumping a corner. The two different routes test communication as the horse may try to anticipate which second element to jump. Accuracy is more important for an angled fence than a straight one as any loss of straightness immediately changes the take-off point.

The horse should have jumped single fences at an angle and related fences off a turn in canter before doing this exercise.

SETTING UP

- Place the fences off the track on the long side, a stride apart. The fences can be jumped individually as part of the warm-up.
- Cross poles are not suitable for angling. The diagram shows an average amount of angle; the fences can be rotated by about 30cm (1ft) either way to decrease or increase the angle. Bear in mind that decreasing the angles for route 1 makes route 2 more difficult.

GETTING STARTED

1 Warm up, and then jump a few easy fences, as shown in diagram A. Jump only in the direction shown to avoid encouraging run-outs when you begin the exercise.

2 Start the exercise using route 1 in diagram B – the side of the arena will help to guide the horse in a straight line.

PROGRESSING

3 When the horse is jumping route 1 easily, progress to route 2. Pinpoint the place to turn off the track for the first element before you make an approach. The correct place to turn is where you can line up the centre of the two fences one directly behind the other. Coloured poles make this easy; otherwise find something beyond the second element to line up with the centre of the first fence. This is the same principle as for lining up a corner.

4 Route 3 involves jumping towards the side of the arena. This will make the horse back off the second element and he may try to stop if he lacks confidence.

5 Combine the routes shown in both diagrams to create a course. The aim is to maintain a constant rhythm and to jump every fence at its centre.

Bits and pieces

- Bitting and saddlery issues can be exposed by changes of pace or tighter turns. Always check the mouth and teeth when changing bits.
- Horses change shape both as they develop and throughout a season. Check your saddle still fits. A regular visit from a physiotherapist is a good investment for any horse competing regularly.
- If you use a martingale, the exercises in this section are good for checking how tight it should be and whether or not you need it at all.

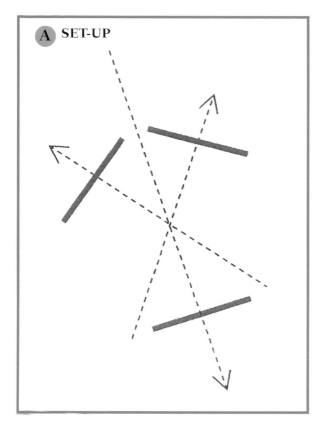

A SET-UP

Place the fences off the track on the long side, a stride apart, and jump them individually.

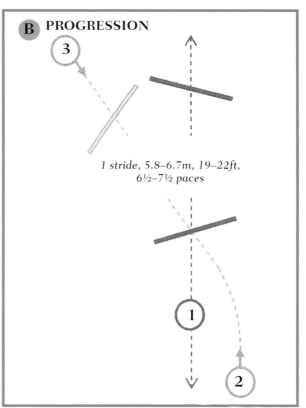

B PROGRESSION

3

1 stride, 5.8–6.7m, 19–22ft, 6½–7½ paces

1

2

Route 3 is harder than 2 because the wall or fence enclosing the arena will encourage the horse to back off the second element.

Changes of pace

- Angles, water, coffins and spooky fences are all examples of fences that require a slower approach.
- The challenge is to **slow down in time to get the leg on and start moving forwards again** at least three strides before the fence. This skill needs practice.
- Much time is lost by slowing down inefficiently before these fences or by taking too long to get up to speed afterwards.
- Stops at such obstacles are often the result of the rider still applying the brakes in the last three strides or being too slow to get the leg on and allow the horse to look at the fence.

How to ride it

- **Keep the horse straight;** do not allow him to jink to one side on take-off.
- **Maintain a good contact** but with a relaxed arm, and keep the leg around the horse without clamping it there.
- **Looking where you want to go is vital for accuracy.** A strategically placed jump block, several strides away from the landing, can help you to get your line.

Fixing common faults

Lack of straightness: The horse must go forwards before he can go straight. If you have placed the horse in a 'vice' between your hand and leg, he is likely to stop thinking forwards. If you tighten up and try to force straightness the horse will also become tense and either hit the fences, dive at them or jink to the side at the slightest opportunity.

CORRECTING YOUR LINE

Top left: The horse is jumping the first part centrally but even so, he is still not straight in his body. This is something that needs working on and this is a very good exercise to encourage that straightness. The rider is doing a very good job of getting the horse on to the right line: she is opening her left rein and looking exactly where she wants to go.

Left: Here the correction is continuing, she is bringing him over to the left on the correct line and supporting him with her right leg. However, you can see how far that crooked jump has brought him off the straight line from middle to middle that I am looking for.

Left: The horse is jumping out confidently – there was never any doubt in his mind as to what he had to do, but he is not as central as I would like to see.

CONTINUING THE CORRECTION

Below right: The horse has not done a bad job of holding his line although there has still been a slight drift to the right coming out. However, he has been straight in his body throughout.

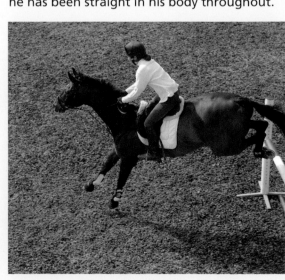

ACHIEVING STRAIGHTNESS

Left: In this sequence, we have got a very good example of this horse staying on a straight line. He is jumping the first fence centrally over the blue section. He has taken a straight stride and is jumping out straight as well, which is the kind of discipline that we need to see in this exercise. It is very important that horses learn to approach on a straight line, jump on that line and move away from the fence without deviating until the rider asks them to turn.

Below: Here again she has him nicely straight and is riding for the stride.

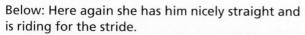

Below: The horse is more central to the first fence than in the top, far left photo, although he still tends to be a little bit crooked in his right shoulder. The jockey is in a very good balanced position and is correcting him.

Narrow fences

Uses

■ To practise a cross-country fence, add variety and hone instinctive reactions

■ To improve accuracy, straightness and communication

■ To practise changes of pace

Unsuitable for

■ Horses unable to jump full-width fences straight

■ Horses that run out at full-width fences

Narrow fences test straightness and communication. Jumping them does not make a horse straight; only work on the flat can achieve that. However, this exercise will improve communication, provided your horse already listens to you, and through that, it will assist straightness. You are aiming for a horse that stays straight out of habit. Using narrow fences in conjunction with other exercises offers an almost limitless variety of options. You can replace fences in another exercise with narrow ones or use them before or after any other jumps. The factors to consider are the narrowness of the obstacle, how spooky it is and what comes before or after it. Narrow fences are great for testing changes of pace – try placing one before or after a spread for example.

This exercise is suitable for anyone, provided you start small and do not try to progress beyond the level of straightness your horse is capable of on the flat.

SETTING UP

■ Build some full-width fences that the horse will find easy as well as the narrow ones.
■ Make narrow fences inviting at first by keeping them low and using wings or poles to lead the horse into the centre of them (diagram A).
■ Narrow fences knock down more easily so it is useful to put up two or three. Avoid lots of open space around the fences to begin with, as that will just encourage run-outs.

GETTING STARTED

1 Warm up, concentrating on straightness and making sure the horse is in front of the leg.
2 Approach in trot until straightness is well established. Vary the type of fence used, as shown in the diagrams.

PROGRESSING

3 Add narrow fences into a situation where the horse is already going forwards and straight – a grid or related distance for example. Make it as easy as possible.
4 Next, use them to test straightness in a situation where that is often lost – after turns or after a change of pace. (Refer to the 'Double of angles' exercise, 'Changes of pace', p. 59).

How to ride it

■ **Whenever accuracy is involved**, there is a great temptation to tense up and try to force the horse to stay straight. The legs should cocoon the horse without him leaning on either one of them. Feel as though three-quarters of the horse is in front of you and use your legs to keep that feeling. When he is 'in front of the leg', the horse actually feels physically wider and higher forwards of your legs, and narrower and lower behind you. Keep the contact but with softness. If you are kicking, you cannot possibly feel the beginnings of any drift to one side or the other. Look where you want to go.
■ **It is important to be going forwards** and not still applying the brakes when approaching any fence at a slower speed.
■ **Stay straight for as long as possible after the fence**, at least three strides to begin with.
■ **Keep your hands slightly wider apart** on the approach to a narrow fence. This will allow you to open the rein quickly to correct any loss of straightness. Teaching your horse to move away from the leg promptly can make the difference between correcting your line successfully and running out. You will not always make a good turn and arrive in the best shape in front of the fence!

Fixing common faults

Running out: You need to be much quicker and firmer to stop a run-out at a narrow fence than at a full-width one. Approach more slowly – in walk if need be, but it must be a forward-going walk! Make sure you get straight before the fence – turn away if you have made a poor turn.

Loss of rhythm: The rhythm will be lost if the horse is not straight and you are using too much hand. Re-establish forward momentum, straightness and rhythm before re-approaching narrow fences.

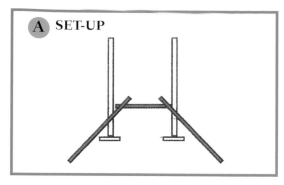

A SET-UP

Make narrow fences inviting at first by keeping them low and using wings or poles to lead the horse into the centre. This stage is suitable for most horses and riders.

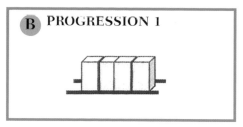

B PROGRESSION 1

If jump blocks are used, they can be removed one at a time, or stacked, to gradually narrow and raise the fence. This stage is for Pre-Novice level and above. Because a line of blocks can be used, they can start to wean the horse off any reliance on wings. Bring the wings back later for more difficult obstacles (diagram C).

C PROGRESSION 2

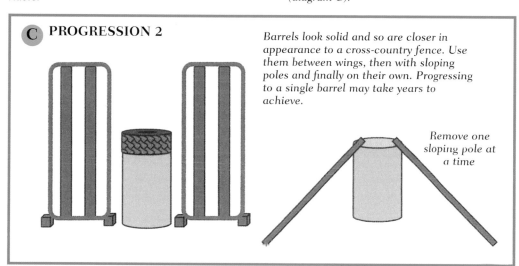

Barrels look solid and so are closer in appearance to a cross-country fence. Use them between wings, then with sloping poles and finally on their own. Progressing to a single barrel may take years to achieve.

Remove one sloping pole at a time

What to use

- Narrow poles, fillers, barrels and jump blocks make good narrow fences. Use as many different types of jump as possible provided that whatever you use will not hurt if the horse stands on it. Introduce a young horse to any unusual obstacles within a full-width fence first – cross one bridge at a time.
- Placing a tyre on top of a barrel protects against sharp edges, makes the fence a reasonable size and looks solid. Avoid tyres on the ground in case the horse puts a foot in the middle of them.

Building trust

- **Move forwards slowly.** Take seamlessly progressive steps so that you only ask the horse reasonable questions. You are aiming for him to approach everything as an interesting new task, not as a challenge to his instincts or as an escape from your dominance. Reward all progress, however small.
- **Do only what you know** is within both of your capabilities. Never attempt something to 'see what happens' unless you know it is within your horse's ability and you are prepared to follow it through. Bear in mind that, like us, what is within a horse's scope on one day may be all too much on another. If you have any doubt about your ability to solve a problem, finish on something easy and seek help before the issue becomes a permanent scar.
- **Get to know your horse** so you know how he is likely to react and are always at least one step ahead of him. This includes knowing when to repeat a task and when to stop. Presenting a horse with something new gives you the chance to learn the sequence of signals he gives out when he is worried. The more attuned you are to the first signs of trouble, the more quickly you can counteract them until eventually you act instinctively. Ultimately, this is the only way you can be quick enough to act – prevention is everything!
- **Give the horse time** to understand something new. Hitting him when he is confused will cause him to associate things he is worried about with additional pain, potentially creating a permanent problem. Stay quiet, make sure he can see what he is doing (back off if you are right in front of the fence) and keep asking. He can safely jump anything below knee height from a standstill, provided he can see it.
- **Use a more experienced horse** to give a youngster a lead. This is often the most efficient way of overcoming any reticence. Stay close behind the lead horse – a length or two is far enough away.
- **Keep moving!** Put the new obstacle into a small course to help keep forward thinking and momentum, and to encourage a good rhythm.
- **Remember that fear** may remain under the surface for a long time. Even if a horse has just jumped something several times, he may still be worried by it. A young horse may take more than a year to accept spooky obstacles as remotely routine.
- **There is security in quiet discipline.** It is a fine line between reassuring the horse and pandering to his unfounded fears to the extent that he has no respect for you. Use your legs to reassure and insist. Tipping forwards and patting him in front of the fence or on landing is unbalancing and is not what you will be doing in front of a bigger jump! He must learn to associate your legs with positive feelings and reassurance.

Pippa Funnell MBE

Introduction to the exercises

The most important thing for the rider to work on is the quality and rhythm of the canter. The following exercises work to improve the canter and to encourage the rider to sit still.

ADVICE TO NEWCOMERS

Be over-prepared, so that the challenge is always reassuringly within your horse's current level of training. Finally, find someone you trust to help you – remember that no rider ever stops learning, and the day they think they have is the day their standards will drop.

Pippa Funnell on Primmore's Pride at the Athens Olympics.

Pippa Funnell is one of the most consistently successful event riders that Britain has ever produced. In 2003 she won Lexington, Badminton and Burghley to become the first winner of the Rolex Grand Slam – the biggest prize in eventing. She holds two Olympic team silver medals and an individual bronze from the Sydney and Athens Olympics. Twice European Champion, she has three European Championship team gold medals and an individual bronze to her name. In 2002 she won team bronze at the World Equestrian Games in Jerez. Three Badminton titles, together with her Grand Slam triumph, place her among the sport's all-time élite.

Pippa became Young Rider European Champion in 1987 and, although several successes followed, the top level eluded her until she integrated sports psychology into her approach. She was the first rider openly to endorse its use, and as a result, it is now universally recognized as an important aid to success.

Pippa has produced two books and three videos covering her training methods and the story of her rise to the top. She is committed to encouraging the riders of the future through clinics, demonstrations and student training via her involvement with the Quest-X challenge. Pippa is married to top show jumper, William Funnell.

More... www.pippa_funnell.com

TRAINING PHILOSOPHY

■ It is my strong belief that building a partnership with a horse is the single most important factor for success. To achieve a strong partnership requires trust, shared enjoyment and the confidence that comes from the horse knowing you will never ask him to do something that is beyond his current capabilities, and from you knowing that he will always do his best for you.

■ One of the most satisfying and fascinating projects you can undertake is to produce a young horse. Although that requires huge reserves of time, patience and perseverance, it is often more rewarding than riding a 'made' horse. However, whether your horse is already made or you are bringing him on yourself, the same principles apply.

■ Training is all about giving the horse confidence by focusing on his strengths rather than his weaknesses. Every horse is different and needs an individual approach but for them to reach the top they must be willing to learn. The work must be progressive so that they find it fun and are never disheartened by being repeatedly asked to do things they find too difficult or frightening or for which they are insufficiently prepared. When there is a setback, it is important to look for the cause and deal with it before the problem multiplies. Equally, you must recognize faults that stem from your riding – it can be just as important to work on yourself as on your horse.

■ I don't just view training as a way to guarantee success, but as a means to producing a confident horse that is safe and well mannered, and gives an enjoyable ride. While it is a great thrill to win at the top level, it can be just as rewarding when a horse at any level shows he has learned something or demonstrates his trust in you.

Introducing stride adjustment

Uses

■ Improves rhythm and the ability to adjust the stride

■ Helps the rider learn to stay still and to see a stride

Unsuitable for

■ Horses and riders who are not practised at shortening and lengthening

This exercise works on rhythm within the different gears (length of stride) in canter. It requires discipline because poles do not command the same level of respect as fences. It is very good for improving the rider as it teaches them to sit still while they adjust the stride, and the poles do not punish the horse for the rider's mistakes. Riding known distances also develops the rider's eye for a stride and enables them to learn their horse's usual stride length. This will help them to recognize distances their horse will find long, short or just right when they walk a course. Awkward distances ride relatively easily when the stride can be altered quickly and smoothly. Once a horse has perfected this skill, he will be better able to get himself out of trouble as well as being more responsive to the aids. All this improves horse and rider confidence. Lastly, it is essential to be able to adjust the stride effectively, without losing rhythm, if you are to achieve consistently clear rounds.

SETTING UP

■ Place the poles on the floor in the middle of the working area so you can work evenly on both reins (see diagram opposite).
■ Use the distances shown as a rough guide. How far apart you place the poles depends on your horse's normal length of stride. You have got it right when you can ride four then another four equal strides easily without any adjustment.

GETTING STARTED

1 Include some transitions and canter shortening and lengthening in your warm-up. Go over one or two of the poles to make sure the canter does not alter over them. The canter must be good before you start, and remain so throughout the exercise.

2 Start by coming level on four and four, then on five and five (or vice versa). 'Level' means all the strides must be of the same length, balance and rhythm. Progress only when you are consistently getting a level four, four and then five, five strides on demand. You are aiming for the horse to relax into the exercise so he listens to you.

3 Ride a straight line through the poles but circle away when necessary to help to shorten the canter and to correct any loss of rhythm and balance.

PROGRESSING

4 Start mixing up the number of strides you ask for. Do four and five or five and four so you learn how quickly you can change the length of stride while maintaining the rhythm.

5 After doing the exercise, you can put the work into context by riding some small individual fences, concentrating on sitting still and keeping the rhythm.

The importance of rhythm

Try riding the most basic circle while going faster and slower, faster and slower. It is extremely difficult to maintain the size of circle and sit still in these circumstances. The rhythm is the foundation of the stride – if it is erratic then the horse cannot balance well or contain his power (engine). When he is in a good rhythm he can comply with his rider's instructions. Conversely, watch a horse with poor rhythm jump; you never know what is going to happen next – a good turn, a poor turn, too close to the fence or standing off a mile. Rhythm provides a constant base from which to build power and better balance. Without good rhythm real control and accuracy are impossible.

How to ride it

- **Sit very still and do not change your seat pressure** the whole way through the exercise.
- **Keep the rhythm by counting**, or by humming a tune to yourself. That makes you aware of the rhythm so that you don't end up slowing down or speeding up. Remember to breathe!
- **To shorten the stride**, sit tall and hold with your seat, back and hands while creating energy with your legs. This will 'concertina' the horse so that you keep the energy in the stride. The hand must never pull back but should remain still as the leg keeps the energy coming forwards.
- **To lengthen**, ease the hand forwards and use both legs to make the stride bigger.
- **You need a good quality canter all the time** – not just through the exercise. The horse must carry himself – if he is leaning on you then that must be worked on first. Visualizing coming into a big fence when you are nowhere near one is one way of focusing your mind on improving the quality of the canter.
- **Allow the horse to canter over the poles unimpeded** – if you alter the stride over them, he will either start to jump them or stand on them.
- **Canter work can be strenuous** – give your horse a break when he does well and watch for any signs that he is tiring.

Fixing common faults

Pushing with the seat: Riders often go wrong in show jumping by pushing too much with their seat on the last few strides. Often the seat is also too heavy and the horse hollows against it. Keep the exercise simple and have someone watch to see if you are moving too much. Work towards sitting more lightly and remaining still without tightening. If you need more energy in the stride, create it with your legs rather than your seat.

Uneven strides: Circle, and work on re-establishing the rhythm. Make sure the distance is comfortable for your horse before you start adjusting the stride. Stick to the same number of strides before and after the central pole until all are of even length, then progress to shortening before the central pole and lengthening after it.

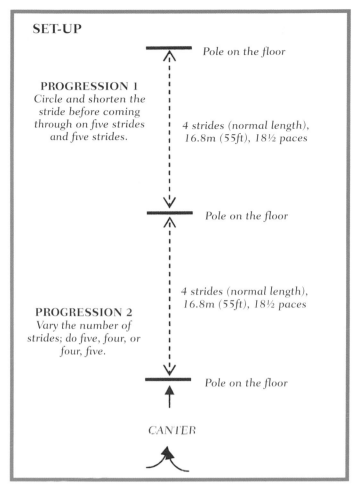

SET-UP

Pole on the floor

PROGRESSION 1
Circle and shorten the stride before coming through on five strides and five strides.

4 strides (normal length), 16.8m (55ft), 18½ paces

Pole on the floor

4 strides (normal length), 16.8m (55ft), 18½ paces

PROGRESSION 2
Vary the number of strides; do five, four, or four, five.

Pole on the floor

CANTER

Set the poles in the middle of the working area. Adjust the distances until you can ride between each pole with four equal strides at your horse's normal stride length.

Even strides over a pole

Below: In the photograph on the right, horse and rider are correctly focusing on the pole, which continues into the next shot where Darrell has allowed the horse to look down at it so he meets it right, in the middle of his stride. The horse looks relaxed and attentive and is taking nice even strides; the first and last ones are the same length. Darrell is sitting very still and quietly with even seat pressure, although his shoulders could be a fraction further back in the first and last shots. This whole sequence is very good.

Advanced stride adjustment

Uses

- Improves rhythm and the ability to adjust the stride
- Helps the rider stay still and to see a stride

Unsuitable for

- Horses and riders who are not practised at shortening and lengthening

This exercise improves the horse and rider's ability to adjust the stride smoothly, quickly and effectively before and after a fence. It teaches the rider to sit quietly and use minimal aids to maximum effect and is a stage on from the previous exercise. Riding the first pole to the central fence tests the ability to keep a consistent level stride as the rider will often be tempted to over-ride a bigger fence. The final pole tests the speed of recovery after the fence, the rider's focus (as this is often lost on landing), and the quality of the canter, which should not change. The first aim is to achieve consistency in the canter throughout the exercise on a comfortable number of strides over a small fence. The ultimate aim is to achieve that consistency whatever the stride pattern, before or after any height of fence.

SETTING UP

- This exercise is best done in a field due to the space needed (see diagram A).
- Set the distances so your horse can do three easy strides before the placing pole and four easy strides after the cross pole.

GETTING STARTED

1 As part of your warm-up, use shortening and lengthening and jump the cross pole before you include the first and last poles.

2 Start the exercise as shown in diagram A. Ride three strides to the placing pole then four strides after the cross pole; you are working on doing nothing and keeping the rhythm. You can vary how many strides you put in as long as you keep it level.

3 Adding canter poles after the first pole can be helpful (diagram B).

4 Remove the placing pole and ride four strides before and after a small vertical.

How to ride it

- **The aim is to sit still and do nothing** but keep the rhythm and quality of the canter. However, in order to do this the horse has to be in self-carriage and in front of the leg. Only then can true rhythm be developed. Getting a certain number of strides between poles is not what is important.
- **Keep the seat pressure constant.** Very often when your eye clicks in and you see your stride, the natural thing is to create slightly more pressure under your seat – so you start very slightly pushing with your bottom. That is why we have to work to keep the seat contact the same the whole way round the corner and to the fence. That links up with sitting still and doing nothing. As soon as you push with your seat it can hollow the horse away from you and that's when the stride can lengthen or quicken.
- **It is helpful to have someone on the ground** watching how still you are sitting, as you may be moving much more than you think you are.

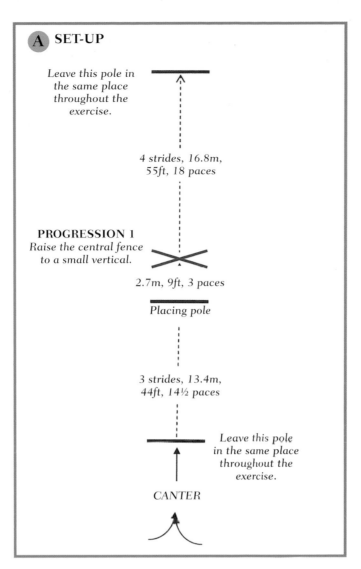

A SET-UP

Leave this pole in the same place throughout the exercise.

4 strides, 16.8m, 55ft, 18 paces

PROGRESSION 1
Raise the central fence to a small vertical.

2.7m, 9ft, 3 paces

Placing pole

3 strides, 13.4m, 44ft, 14½ paces

Leave this pole in the same place throughout the exercise.

CANTER

Canter poles

■ Using canter poles makes the horse take deliberate strides over each one. That gives him a definite rhythm and you don't have to interfere with that. Then once you take the poles away you just have to think of the same sort of rhythm.

■ The poles can also help you to recognize even stride lengths by feel and they help the horse to develop even strides.

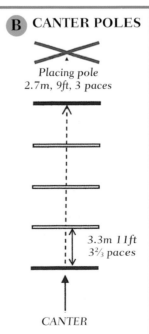

B CANTER POLES

Placing pole
2.7m, 9ft, 3 paces

3.3m 11ft
3⅔ paces

CANTER

Add three poles (marked in grey) between the first pole and the placing pole. Leave the pole on the landing side as it is.

PROGRESSING

4 Build a small spread only when you can maintain the rhythm and vary the strides either side of the vertical without over-riding the canter. It may take time to achieve a good canter on a different number of strides. Progress only when the quality of the canter allows: there is no benefit in constantly creating a stilted or flat stride.

5 Square the oxer before raising it because an ascending spread would encourage the horse to jump out further, making the task unnecessarily more difficult.

6 Start with four strides before and after the oxer.

7 Then do five short strides before it, followed by four after it. The four strides should be relatively easy.

8 After that, it is up to you to vary the exercise depending on your progress. Between three and five strides are possible either side of the oxer. However, it is more difficult to do longer strides before the oxer and shorter strides after it. The challenge then, on landing, is to sit up and shorten the canter in time to keep the strides level, without unbalancing the canter by applying the aids too abruptly or forcefully.

Canter quality

■ The most important thing for the rider to work on is the quality and rhythm of the canter so that the horse has every chance of meeting fences in balance and therefore jumping them well. He must carry himself without you having him too pressurized between hand and leg.

■ A horse can only ever be a maximum of half a stride wrong for a fence so the more engaged and balanced the canter is, the easier it is to make any slight adjustment necessary, whether that means slightly gaining ground or losing ground.

■ Half a stride wrong over four or five strides does not require a major adjustment. This is where most riders get it wrong because they either over-hook or move the horse on too much. That half stride can easily be gained or lost over four strides – sometimes enough difference can be made just by sitting up a little bit more with your body.

Shortening the canter

■ **Keep the energy but with less pace.** Think of riding forwards without thinking speed. The engagement comes from activating the hind leg to bring it underneath the horse – never by pulling backwards. I use my upper body and balance as much as anything else to shorten the canter.

■ **Sit lightly and *allow* the energy to come upwards** through your body; otherwise the horse will get tense and start to think 'what do you want?'. There has to be softness in your body and even though you sit up very tall, you must also sit lightly so that the horse's back can come up. This enables his hind leg to come underneath him. If you sit too heavy, there is nowhere for that energy to go so the horse tightens: he cannot move the energy forwards, as speed, because you are shortening.

■ **Generate more power and bounce in the stride** by keeping a steady contact to contain the energy your leg creates. It has all got to be soft in the way that the horse carries himself and he comes upwards.

■ **Remember that it takes a considerable amount of training** for the horse to develop enough strength to be able to achieve collection, so do not try to force a shorter stride than he is capable of producing.

■ **The horse should be able to shorten and lengthen all in the same rhythm.**

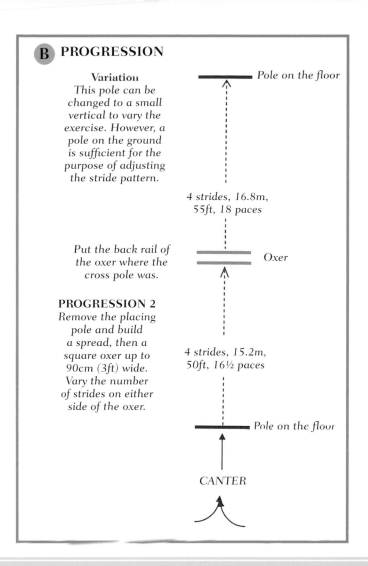

B PROGRESSION

Variation
This pole can be changed to a small vertical to vary the exercise. However, a pole on the ground is sufficient for the purpose of adjusting the stride pattern.

Pole on the floor

4 strides, 16.8m, 55ft, 18 paces

Put the back rail of the oxer where the cross pole was.

Oxer

PROGRESSION 2
Remove the placing pole and build a spread, then a square oxer up to 90cm (3ft) wide. Vary the number of strides on either side of the oxer.

4 strides, 15.2m, 50ft, 16½ paces

Pole on the floor

CANTER

Fixing common faults

All faults for the previous exercise also apply to this one.

Achieving fewer strides than intended after the fence: Make sure you are not collapsing on landing – look up while in the air to guard against this. Check your lower leg does not move back. Apply your shortening aids as soon as your horse lands. Halt before the final pole if the horse is speeding up.

Hitting the back rail: The horse must land before you start shortening the stride.

Hitting the front rail: Check that you are not pushing with the seat, restricting the horse on take-off or getting in front of the movement. You may be getting too deep to the fence by asking for too many strides before it. Or, the horse may be flattening because the stride has become long and flat.

Stride lengths and take-off points

- The normal length of stride for a horse is 3–3.7m (10–12ft). A lengthened stride will be 3.9–4.5m (13–15ft) and a shortened one 2.1–2.7m (7–9ft).
- A horse will usually take off 1.4m (4ft 6in) in front of a small fence or 1.8m (6ft) in front of one 1.1m (3ft 6in) or above. When going over a single pole on the floor, he should take a normal length stride, with the pole in the middle of the stride.

Jane Holderness-Roddam CBE LVO

Of special importance to Jane

★*Winning Badminton on Our Nobby and going to the Olympics in the same year was an amazing experience as I was training as a nurse at the Middlesex Hospital at that time. Selection for the Olympics was more like a fairy tale, but would not have been achieved without the help of my family, friends and the co-operation of the hospital.*

★*Winning Burghley in 1976 and Badminton in 1978 – both on Warrior. I was very lucky to have a second great horse and it was thanks to his American owner, Suzie Howard, who bought him for me to ride, that I was able to have a second run of successes.*

★*Top trainers: I was also particularly lucky to have had such wonderful help over many years, especially from my sister, Jennie Loriston-Clarke, Dick Stillwell, Iris Kellet, Gunnar Andersen, Ernst Bachinger, Bert de Nemethy, Bertie Hill, Pat Burgess and Lady Hugh Russell, all of whom taught me so much in many different ways.*

Few people can have achieved so much for their sport as Jane Holderness-Roddam has for eventing. She was the first British woman to compete in the Olympic three-day event, winning team gold in Mexico in 1968 on the 15hh Our Nobby. She won Badminton twice and Burghley, and gained team gold at the European Championships. Jane was the first woman to chair British Eventing and her advice on all aspects of the sport is highly sought after. As a judge, trainer, steward and technical delegate she gives extensive practical support to the event world. Together with her husband, Tim, she is committed to the worldwide promotion of British Sport Horse breeding. West Kington Stud is at the cutting edge of artificial insemination, ensuring the quality of the next generation of eventers. Jane is the author of over 20 books covering all elements of care and training from showing to eventing, and is Chairman of the Riding for the Disabled Association and the National Riding Festival. She is President of British Eventing, the British Equestrian Trade Association (BETA) and the Fortune Centre of Riding Therapy (FCRT).

More...www.westkingtonstud.co.uk

TRAINING PHILOSOPHY

■ My general philosophy is to build up the confidence between horse and rider to enable them to realize their aims and ambitions. To achieve this, I believe there are three basic requirements, *forwardness*, *straightness* and *balance*, to enable a combination to progress from correct flatwork preparation so that they can jump successfully at whatever level. A certain degree of each is essential and all are relevant to each other. Without the horse going forwards from the leg into the contact, it will be difficult to achieve true straightness. Without straightness, it will be difficult to maintain balance. If the horse is not in balance, it will be unable to perform even quite simple exercises satisfactorily.

ADVICE TO NEWCOMERS

Be really dedicated in your approach, and be sure you and the horse understand the basics of shortening and lengthening the stride, then everything falls into place. Always have the horse going forwards from the leg into a light hand contact. Whatever you do, pay attention to detail and be confident in your approach to everything.

Introduction to the exercises

The following exercises are designed to help horse and rider to communicate more effectively and to teach the horse to respond to the rider's aids. They help the co-ordination of both to respond to a shorter or longer stride as necessary, yet maintain balance throughout.

Jane Holderness-Roddam on Warrior at Badminton.

Circles for suppleness and accustoming horses to poles

Uses

- To improve suppleness, co-ordination and balance

Unsuitable for

- Inexperienced riders unable to keep true rhythm and balance; it may be a stage too far to undertake in trot. However, at walk, this exercise can be useful for all horses and riders

This exercise helps suppleness, co-ordination and balance, and teaches the rider to use legs, seat and hands independently. You are aiming to achieve a forward rhythm over the poles, suppleness on the turns, and elevation through the shoulders and haunches as the horse steps over the poles. All of which will improve the way the horse uses himself and will therefore enhance his ability to turn and to jump. Poles on the ground are used in many jumping exercises so it is essential to familiarize the horse with them.

Some people find this exercise easy to do, others find it remarkably difficult to work out the sequence, even though they may be experienced riders. Generally, I find I need to walk through the exercise on foot in front of the riders to explain what is required in the first instance.

SETTING UP

- You require six poles – fairly heavy ones of a uniform length are best – set 3m (10ft) apart in the centre of the arena or training area (diagram A).

GETTING STARTED

1 This exercise is useful for any horse, regardless of its age or ability, but initially youngsters should only do it in walk as it is relatively strenuous on young limbs.

2 The horse should be introduced to the line by walking, then trotting straight through it.

PROGRESSING

3 Once the horse is happy and relaxed at walk through the poles, ask for a 3–5m circle to the right over the first pole, then move on to circle to the left over the second pole and on down to the right over the third, then left and so on to the end (see diagram A).

4 Be consistent with the size of the circles, but do not force the horse, who must be relaxed to achieve the necessary suppleness.

5 A variation is to circle on the same rein all the way down, then change the rein.

6 Once you have done this in walk, you can progress to doing it at trot (see diagram B). Initially, start over two poles in a circle to the right, then two to the left, then the final two to the right. Repeat on the other rein.

7 Remember this is a tiring exercise so do not overdo it – two or three times in both directions is usually enough. Finish on a good note.

How to ride it

- **The secret is to keep the circles of a uniform size** throughout so that the horse can circle with ease and then keep moving actively forwards. It is important to keep turning over the centre and round the edge of each pole and continue walking actively from start to finish. In trot, keep the size uniform.
- **The rider must maintain the forwardness** and assess a suitable speed to ensure there is enough impulsion to maintain good balance and rhythm throughout.
- **It is vital that the rider 'allows' the horse to turn** on the circle by very slightly easing the outside rein forwards, but never crossing it over the wither, which would completely 'block' the horse's ability to move freely forwards.

Fixing common faults

Extreme stiffness on one or both reins: Most faults, such as extreme stiffness on one or both reins, will become very apparent during this exercise. Start in walk and progress into a steady, slow trot as the horse loosens up. It is important the horse is not pushed out of his rhythm, which will tend to make him even tighter and more tense. Work evenly on both reins – do not be tempted to overwork on the worst rein. It takes time to change the way the horse's muscles are developed.

Lack of impulsion or response to the rider's aids: A long whip may be very helpful in flicking the horse's hind end to become more engaged and active, particularly with the lazy type of horse.

A SET-UP

2.7–3m, 9–10ft,
3–3⅓ paces

Walk over the first pole and circle RIGHT, then walk over the second and circle LEFT.

3–5m, 10–16½ft circle

WALK

B PROGRESSION

Turn between each set of two poles. For example: trot over the first two to the right, then on over 3 and 4 to the left and 5 and 6 to the right.

Count 'One, two, turn and ...', then move up to the next two poles.

2.7–3m, 9–10ft,
3–3⅓ paces

6–8m, 20–26ft circle

TROT

Place the poles in the centre of the working area and walk or trot straight through them.

Trot through the exercise, circling two poles at a time.

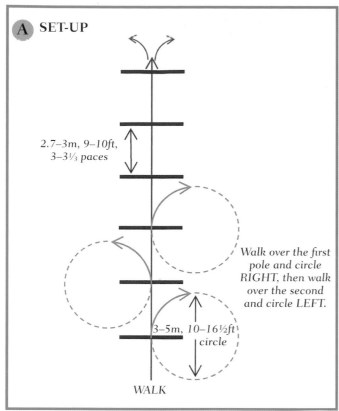

Antoinette is walking over the fourth pole to the right and allowing the outside hand to go forwards a little so that the horse can bend from her outside leg to her inside hand in a small circle over the centre of the poles.

Marcus has already done his first circle to the left in trot and is now moving down to poles three and four to commence his circle to the right.

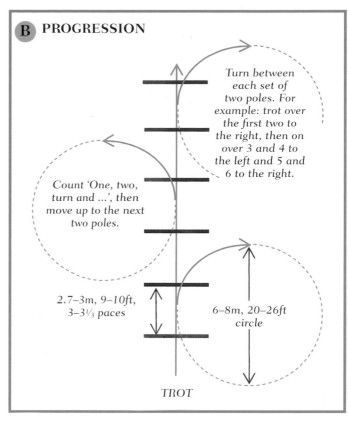

Here she is continuing the circle movement. The horse has perhaps got a little bit long but is turning quite nicely round to come over the centre of the pole before changing the bend.

Throughout the turn, Marcus is using his outside leg and softening his outside hand so that the horse can complete its circle over poles three and four. They will then change direction over the last two poles.

As they come over the centre of the pole and begin to circle to the left, you can see that the horse is obviously a little bit stiffer this way as his head has come up. He is going to have to work quite hard to get round in a balanced circle to reach the centre of the pole again.

The last of the two poles to circle. Here the horse is picking up nicely over the pole and looks more balanced than in the first photograph as he has started to get the right idea about the exercise.

Circling poles in canter

Uses

■ Co-ordination, suppleness, balance and accuracy

Unsuitable for

■ Very young horses or those without an established canter

■ Horses that cannot canter a 12m circle

■ Horses with known physical problems or that are not fit enough

This exercise works on developing rhythm and balance in the canter and a disciplined approach to working in a confined space. The exercise can be tailored for horses of all standards, once their canter is well established, by selecting the number of poles to circle. The smaller the circle, the more collected the canter must become. Developing a good collected canter will build up the hind end, which is the horse's engine; more power to his 'engine' gives the horse more spring. The canter is the most important pace for jumping horses and it is essential that the rider is able to shorten and lengthen the stride with ease and without resistance if a fluent jumping round is to be achieved.

SETTING UP

■ Place six poles on the ground, centrally in your schooling area. Allow enough room to perform a large circle around all of them (diagram A).

■ Space the poles evenly 2.7–3m (9-10ft) apart.

GETTING STARTED

1 As part of your warm-up, canter around all six poles. Including some lengthening and shortening at this stage will help prepare the horse to produce the necessary collection for the circles.

2 To start the exercise, move within the poles and work between the first and last (diagram A).

3 As a general guide, once the idea is mastered, a young novice horse should be capable of working around three to four poles (diagram A), an Intermediate horse around two to three poles (diagram B), and an Advanced horse around one to two poles (diagram C).

PROGRESSING

4 Establish a true, three-beat canter and work on the rhythm and balance within a larger circle before attempting a smaller circle around fewer poles (diagram B).

5 One smaller circle may be enough initially before returning to a larger circle.

6 This exercise can be quite strenuous, so limit your training sessions to three or four circles on each rein.

How to ride it

■ **Establish balance and control** by creating enough impulsion from the leg up into your hand to maintain an even rhythm. If the strides are too long and the horse is on the forehand, the exercise is virtually impossible. However, if the right degree of balance is established, it becomes easy, even with a relatively green horse.

■ **Keep the rhythm and balance of the stride constant.** Only the pace (speed) may increase or decrease as required.

■ **Do not force the exercise** – it cannot be achieved at any size of circle if the canter is tight and the horse tense. Work on a circle with which your horse is comfortable on both reins.

Fixing common faults

Inability of the horse to work evenly on both reins: Initially, it may not be possible to work round the same number of poles on both reins, especially if the horse tends to be more stiff on one rein. This will improve as he gets stronger and more established in his work.

Basic canter faults: All basic canter faults will show up with this exercise; falling in, stiffness, wrong bend, changing canter leads and so on. Developing suppleness and balance will ultimately correct these, but it is important to keep the horse calm and ride the circles accurately.

Persistent one-sidedness by the horse: If the horse finds the circles difficult on a particular rein after a reasonable period of time, you should consider if there is another reason; for example back or teeth problems, which may need attention.

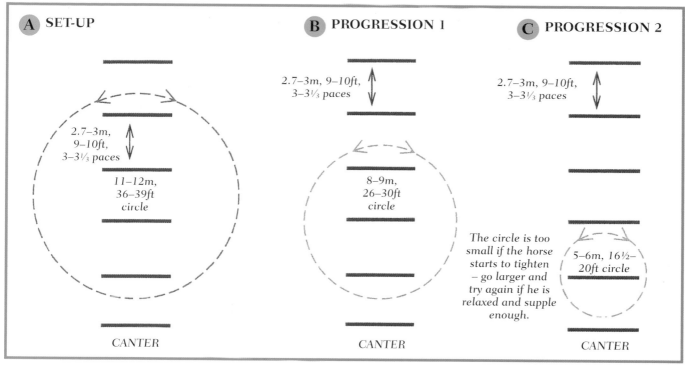

| **A** SET-UP | **B** PROGRESSION 1 | **C** PROGRESSION 2 |

A SET-UP

2.7–3m,
9–10ft,
3–3⅓ paces

11–12m,
36–39ft
circle

CANTER

B PROGRESSION 1

2.7–3m, 9–10ft,
3–3⅓ paces

8–9m,
26–30ft
circle

CANTER

C PROGRESSION 2

2.7–3m, 9–10ft,
3–3⅓ paces

The circle is too small if the horse starts to tighten – go larger and try again if he is relaxed and supple enough.

5–6m, 16½–20ft circle

CANTER

Place six poles in the centre of the working area and canter round them at a size comfortable for your horse's stage of training.

Circle around fewer poles, provided the horse remains balanced, relaxed and is physically capable.

Circling around a single pole in canter is an advanced exercise and requires a very collected, balanced canter.

An unbalanced canter around two poles. The horse has failed to get around the pole because the horse and rider are not together. The rider probably has her reins too long to do this size circle. I would expect her to shorten the canter stride, shorten her reins and get the horse a little bit more balanced before attempting this smaller circle.

A balanced canter around three poles. The rider is nicely balanced and is looking to her route between the first and second pole. She is improving the canter by working on this size circle before she extends it around four poles again. She will then come back to circling three poles before attempting to do two.

Jumping on a figure of eight

Uses

■ Control, rhythm and lead changes

■ Co-ordination and responsiveness of both horse and rider

Unsuitable for

■ Young horses that are not yet established in canter

This exercise establishes control, rhythm and the ability to change leading legs in the air over a fence. It also teaches horse and rider versatility and co-ordination, and how to have the horse on the aids. In addition, it helps to achieve balance and flow, particularly useful on show-jumping courses and especially important if the flying change has not been mastered. The horse must be sufficiently confident at cantering over a course of fences before doing this exercise. It is a natural progression of 'Circling poles in canter'.

SETTING UP

■ It is very easy to set up this exercise: all that is required is a single fence (or pole on the ground) in the middle of the arena along the centre line (see diagram).

■ The fence need not be very big. It should be of a suitable size for the horse's stage of training.

GETTING STARTED

1 The horse needs to be well warmed up and to have jumped some straightforward fences before starting.

2 Start the exercise by jumping two or three times over the fence on the same rein to establish a good flowing rhythm before moving on to the figure of eight.

PROGRESSING

3 Change the rein in canter over the fence and continue on the figure of eight for two or three repetitions before having a break.

4 The fence can be made into a small oxer to increase the width and technicality. Ensure that it can be safely jumped from both directions.

5 The oxer can be gradually raised in height and width for more experienced combinations. It is the technique of opening the rein to the side that is important. The outside rein must allow the bend but never cross over the wither and block the movement.

How to ride it

- **The circles should be consistent in size** and large enough to ensure it is easy to change direction over the fence. In a 20 x 40m (65 x 130ft) arena, a 20m (65ft) circle is a good starting point.
- **The rider should change direction when in the air** by taking the hand out slightly sideways but never pulling backwards with it. This encourages the horse to land on the opposite leg, ready to perform the second circle on the other canter lead.
- **This exercise is best practised** continuously for two or three complete figures of eight before having a break, then repeating it if there have been any problems.

Fixing common faults

Lack of balance and consistency in the circles: This can be corrected by riding from the inside leg into the outside hand throughout the circle.

Horse fails to change its canter lead over the fence: Use a more accentuated new inside hand aid by bringing the hand further away from the neck and guiding the horse on to the other lead. The change of lead can also be helped by a slight shifting of the rider's weight into the stirrup of the new inside leg.

Horse becomes unbalanced on landing: It is important that the change is subtle over the fence, so as not to unbalance the horse.

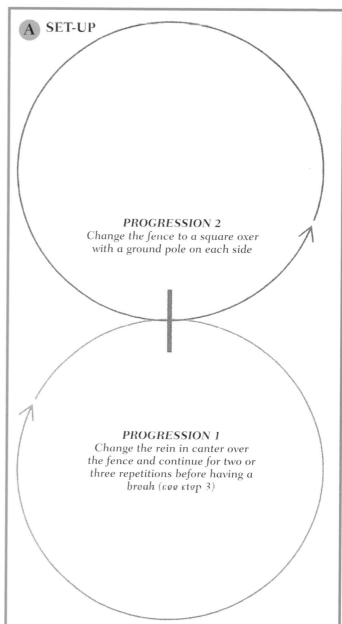

A **SET-UP**

PROGRESSION 2
Change the fence to a square oxer with a ground pole on each side

PROGRESSION 1
Change the rein in canter over the fence and continue for two or three repetitions before having a break (see step 3)

Place a simple vertical fence across the centre line. The fence does not have to be very big. Begin by jumping two or three times in the same direction.

Far left: Darrell is completing a right-handed circle towards the fence in a balanced canter. He is getting ready to change direction in the air over the obstacle.

Middle: As he goes over the fence, he can plainly be seen taking his left hand out to start the left-handed circle. He is allowing the horse to bend by softening his outside hand.

Left: The horse's head is already looking to the left and he has landed on the left lead, ready to circle in that direction. Notice the softness in the rider's hand and the confidence on the horse's face.

Jane Holderness-Roddam

Offset central fence

Jane Holderness-Roddam

Uses
- Improves obedience, balance and suppleness
- Develops instinctive reactions

Unsuitable for
- Very inexperienced horses and riders

This exercise is excellent to help teach riders how use their hands and legs independently: a useful reminder to top riders as well as novices. It is a great favourite with children and can be done by any level of horse or rider, so long as the angle remains suitable for the experience of the rider concerned. It can also be very useful for the horse that rushes or does not turn well, as the changes of direction will confuse the horse which should quickly start to listen to the rider's commands. It develops the ability of horse and rider to react instinctively in the right way.

This exercise can be done by all riders but is best done with horses that are jumping small courses confidently and are ready to do grids and exercises.

SETTING UP
- Three small single fences are required on a straight line with the middle element pulled in off the track at an angle suitable for the ability of horse and rider (see diagram A).
- The central fence should remain small and the whole exercise can be performed over small fences but remain very effective.
- It is often best to start this exercise in trot and with a relatively slight degree of angle depending on the experience of the combination.
- Single fences should be used, rather than spreads.

GETTING STARTED

1 The horse should be warmed up over straightforward fences.

2 A good way to start this exercise is by jumping the first two fences on the diagonal (routes 1 and 2, diagram A) to accustom the horse to approaching at an angle. Return to this stage if problems arise at any time.

3 The middle fence can also be lowered if necessary or even placed on the ground until the change of direction is mastered.

PROGRESSING

4 Put all three elements together (diagram B) and ride the exercise on both reins.

5 Do not do too much in one go, but practise this exercise fairly regularly, gradually increasing the angle and, for an experienced combination, the height also.

6 Reduce the distance between the elements from 2–3 strides to 1–2 strides (diagram B) and raise the fences as appropriate for the experience of horse and rider, but keep the central fence small.

Right: Here the rider is demonstrating what happens when you fail to allow the horse to bend towards the last fence. The outside rein is held too tightly with the result that the horse's head has come up, making for an uncomfortable exit.

How to ride it

- **The secret is to be able to turn** the horse's head with the inside rein over the central fence and ride towards the third element without restricting the head with the outside rein. The rider's hands must follow the head direction with a soft sideways pull, but should never pull backwards, which will raise the head rather than change the direction.
- **Maintain a consistent pace** whether in trot or canter.
- **Keep the pace balanced** out of the corner on the approach and through a controlled turn after the fences.

Fixing common faults

Rider shifting weight and pulling the head up: Watch that the rider keeps a soft hand and never pulls the horse's head upwards or fixes the outside hand preventing a change of direction. The rider must remain central and not shift the weight, which would put strain on to the leading leg. It is the position of the inside hand supported by the outside leg which indicates the change of direction to the horse.

A SET-UP

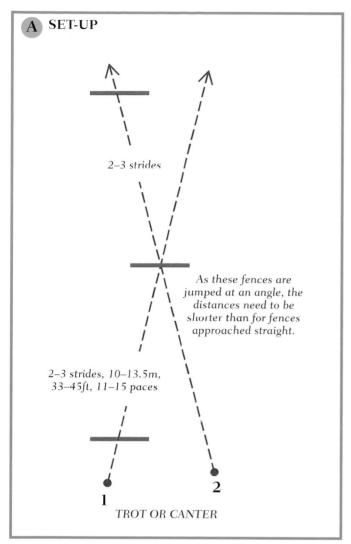

2–3 strides

As these fences are jumped at an angle, the distances need to be shorter than for fences approached straight.

2–3 strides, 10–13.5m, 33–45ft, 11–15 paces

1 **2**

TROT OR CANTER

B

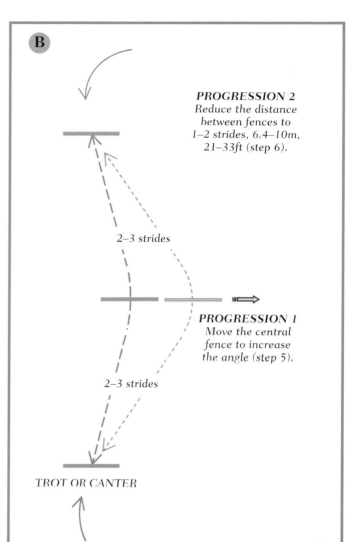

PROGRESSION 2
Reduce the distance between fences to 1–2 strides, 6.4–10m, 21–33ft (step 6).

2–3 strides

PROGRESSION 1
Move the central fence to increase the angle (step 5).

2–3 strides

TROT OR CANTER

Place three fences, as shown, near the side of the working area. The second element is best without wings. Ride the fences individually, then as shown. Begin on the horse's softest rein.

Put all three elements together and ride the exercise on both reins (step 4).

Now the horse has begun to realize what the exercise is all about and is listening to his rider. She is able to turn him over the fence by taking her hand out to the side and the horse is attentive.

A more experienced horse over a bigger fence, showing the horse in perfect harmony with his rider on the turn.

Mary King

Mary King is an Olympic team silver medallist and the holder of one World and four European team gold medals. She has won Badminton twice and has represented Britain at four Olympics. She gained team silver in Athens, despite having broken her neck three years before. Mary is one of the most popular eventing competitors, especially among younger fans to whom she is always ready to give her time.

Favourite achievements

★*My first win at Badminton horse trials was the highlight of my career. It was clearing the last show jump and knowing that I had actually won. I had been lucky enough to be second and third in previous years but to win was just in a league of its own – and to think that I had done it and beaten the rest of the world! It was an event that from a child I just dreamt of trying to get to one day and there I was, many years later, actually winning it.*

★*Getting my first pony, 'Butterboy', was also very special. I had non-horsey parents and begged and borrowed horses but always wanted one of my own. When I was 13, Mum and Dad gave in!*

TRAINING PHILOSOPHY

■ My main aim is to gain the horse's trust and understanding so he can enjoy his work. When I am training young horses, I try to be very clear about what is right or wrong. I am methodical in correcting mistakes, and very quick to reward and encourage horses when they do it correctly. That is my main thing and once they learn that, and it is clear in their minds, then they can go on and enjoy what they are doing. If they are in a bit of a muddle, then they won't and they won't progress!

■ If they do something wrong, they must know that to help them in the future. If they run out, for example, it is very important to stop them immediately, give them a smack, turn them back and growl at them – to make it obvious to them that it is incorrect. Then, when they do it correctly, you must be very ready to reward them with your voice and a pat.

■ What is right or wrong must be black and white. Never ignore little mistakes and think, 'Oh well, next time they will do it right'. That makes it a little bit unclear in their minds as to what they can get away with. They are like children really – constantly trying to stretch the boundaries! You just need to keep them in a corridor but allow them to enjoy themselves as well – they must be encouraged to be happy.

ADVICE TO NEWCOMERS

Follow your dreams, kick on and be positive!

Introduction to the exercises

These are exercises I use most often with my horses. Over the years, having worked with many different trainers, you pick bits out to use yourself, and in the end, these are some of the exercises I use most frequently.

Exercises are a very important part of training a horse; it is vital to get the basics right and secure. You need a broad base to build on to progress to the top level, and training exercises are very much part of forming this.

Mary King on Call Again Cavalier at Gatcombe

Canter shortening and lengthening exercise

Uses
- Improves balance, athleticism, rhythm and communication

Unsuitable for
- This exercise suits most horses

This exercise helps to train the horse to shorten and lengthen his stride and adjust it smoothly and obediently. You are aiming to ride into every fence on a medium-length stride so that your horse can shorten or lengthen it as necessary. The more athletic your horse is, and the more difference there is between your horse's longest and shortest stride, the more likely he is to be able to get you out of trouble when you make a mistake. This exercise also helps to improve communication by teaching the horse to respond to your shortening or lengthening aids. You need to be able to collect the horse *quickly* and smoothly during both show-jumping and cross-country rounds or you will lose valuable time and upset the horse's balance and rhythm. The exercise enables you to see instantly whether your aids are sufficiently effective. To achieve a given number of strides between the two elements, the strides must be even, rhythmic and calm.

SETTING UP

- Place the poles, or verticals, in the centre of your working area, allowing plenty of space to approach on a straight line and get away on a straight line.
- Set the poles so that five strides are easy from your normal medium-length canter stride. This is not the same as *medium canter* which requires a lengthened stride.

GETTING STARTED

1 Warm up by going large around the arena, shortening before the short sides, lengthening as you reach the long sides. Use decreasing and increasing sized circles to help engage the hocks and shorten the canter.

2 Start by using poles. This enables you to concentrate solely on the canter without worrying about the fences. Change the rein each time, beginning with your horse's softest rein. The horse should canter over the centre of the poles without jumping them.

3 Lengthen the stride regularly throughout the exercise so that the horse keeps thinking forwards. The long sides are a good place to do this. If you have a small arena, build the fences up the long side to give you more space.

PROGRESSING

4 When you can maintain a rhythmic five strides between the poles, make them into jumps. Use a straight-bar rather than a cross for the second element so as not to punish your horse if he gets too close and jumps at an angle.

5 Next, shorten the canter to add an extra stride. Gradually add strides then move on quietly to lengthen again, taking out strides one by one. Keep adding extra strides or removing them. Eventually you are aiming to be able to do either four, five, six or seven strides on the same distance.

6 If your horse can easily change lead over the second fence, that's great. However, this is not a suitable exercise for teaching your horse to change lead because you do not want to unbalance him and undo all your hard work! Generally, it is best to teach him one thing at a time.

With a young horse, if he lands on the wrong lead for the next corner, either do a flying change or, if those are not established yet, change legs through trot.

How to ride it

- **Always do shortening first**, before you do lengthening. You need to create a coiled spring effect, otherwise your lengthening will be very flat. The aim is to make the stride bigger, containing the energy, not flatter, dispersing it.

- **Look ahead** when riding over the poles, not down at them. Where you look affects your horse's balance.

- **To shorten the stride**, draw your upper body back and use half-halts to contain the energy you create with your legs.

Fixing common faults

Losing rhythm: Circle to re-establish the canter before returning to the exercise. It is important to keep the rhythm all the way around the arena, not just through the poles.

Unable to shorten: If your horse is very on his forehand and therefore heavy in your hand, then you may find it easier to start the exercise using verticals rather than poles. This can have the effect of backing him off the fence and therefore automatically shortening his stride. Again, circling will help to bring his hocks further underneath him, making shortening possible.

Unable to lengthen: Make sure you have created enough energy by shortening first. Move your hands forwards with every stride to encourage him to take bigger steps. The horse must learn to be sensitive to your leg – a sharp nudge will be needed (with a soft hand) if he is being lazy – reward with your voice or a pat if he responds well.

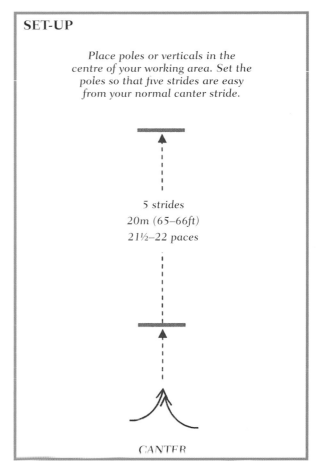

SET-UP

Place poles or verticals in the centre of your working area. Set the poles so that five strides are easy from your normal canter stride.

5 strides
20m (65–66ft)
21½–22 paces

CANTER

Far left: **Collection** *The horse is staying soft and submissive and Darrell has condensed the horse's stride.*

Left: **Lengthening** *Darrell is moving the horse forwards, opening the stride and covering more ground. The stride is becoming bigger and rounder rather than getting quicker and flatter.*

Canter a figure of eight over a vertical and an oxer

Uses
- Improves turns, steering and focus

Unsuitable for
- This exercise suits most horses

This exercise requires frequent changes of rein and therefore tests the ability to turn well. The rider must be accurate because riding a fence across the diagonal is harder than riding one positioned on the long side: it is all too easy to turn too early or too late and once you arrive at the fence, there are no walls to discourage a run-out. Constantly riding from one fence to the next is good practice for riding a course and testing the rider's focus. The combination of oxer and vertical brings its own problems to the equation. An oxer (ascending spread or parallel) requires more effort from the horse and can make him harder to turn on landing. Hence, more space is allowed for the turn after it. A vertical can encourage the horse to get too close on take-off and 'prop' over the fence. With two different types of fence, maintaining rhythm and balance in the canter becomes that much more difficult. The smaller circle after the vertical gives the rider the opportunity to contain the energy in a shorter stride, ready to be released over the oxer.

SETTING UP

- Place the two fences across the diagonals in the centre of the arena (see diagram opposite).

GETTING STARTED

1 The horse and rider must be able to jump fences on the long sides accurately before doing this exercise. To get the most out of it, you should be able to do the exercise on pages 84–5.

2 If you use poles on the ground instead of jumps, use a single pole in place of the oxer. This is a good way to practise turns but the necessary changes of lead are less likely to occur naturally over poles set in this position.

3 Start with small fences (cross poles, for example) so you can concentrate on the turns and changes of lead. Jump the first fence and ride at least one complete circle after it. Then ride the second fence and again, circle afterwards. The aim is to set a calm and constant rhythm and encourage the horse to be balanced. There is no point in putting the fences up or linking them together if you are resorting to pulling your horse around the circle after the jump.

4 Make the second jump an ascending oxer (spread) and circle after it, as before.

5 This exercise is strenuous. Give the horse a break from time to time by a rest or by allowing him to canter on around the arena.

Daisy is in a good position and is already starting to look to the left, where she is going to go.

She is riding smoothly around the turn with her eyes focused firmly on the oxer.

PROGRESSING

6 Link the fences together and ride them solely in the direction shown in the diagram.

7 Square the oxer (make a parallel) to encourage the horse to bascule.

8 Build up the size of the fences, and increase the width of the oxer.

9 Reduce the size of the turn after the fence but ensure the horse is straight on take-off.

How to ride it

- **Notice where changes occur** to the rhythm, balance or impulsion and prevent them from happening.
- **Look for the next fence** as early as possible to help get you on to the right line and facilitate the change of lead.
- **Do not go too far away from the fences** or you will lose the benefit of the turn itself.

Fixing common faults

Losing rhythm: Circle to re-establish the canter before returning to the exercise.

Unbalanced on the turns: Are the fences too big? Did you prepare for the turn sufficiently? Is your horse tired?

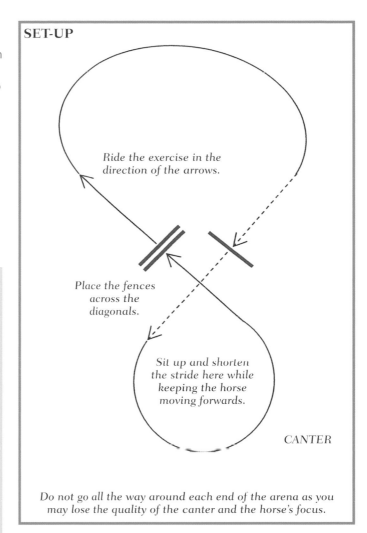

SET-UP

Ride the exercise in the direction of the arrows.

Place the fences across the diagonals.

Sit up and shorten the stride here while keeping the horse moving forwards.

CANTER

Do not go all the way around each end of the arena as you may lose the quality of the canter and the horse's focus.

Jump the vertical, circle left then jump the oxer.

Here she is already looking to the right in preparation for her turn after the fence.

Having landed over the oxer, Daisy is preparing for the turn to the vertical. The horse is looking well balanced but Daisy could have straightened her upper body a little to help the turn.

Canter exercise angling separate elements of a treble

Uses

- Improves accuracy, steering and agility

Unsuitable for

- This exercise will be difficult for a horse that does not go forwards and straight

Eventing requires the horse to jump with pinpoint accuracy – this exercise helps to hone that skill. Your steering will be tested by this exercise, as you will only be successful if you use your legs and seat together with your hands to guide your horse through it. It will improve the horse's general agility and his confidence in making an angled approach to a fence. It will also help to build up the trust between you and your horse.

Your horse must be able to jump the middle of fences when they are approached straight, before you attempt any at an angle.

SETTING UP

- Place the fences in the centre of the arena and use a ground pole on each side of them so they are jumpable from either direction.
- It is best not to use cross poles for this exercise as it is easy to miss the middle of the fence and you do not want to end up hitting the higher part. Preferably, use coloured poles as the stripes will help you to find the middle of the fence.

GETTING STARTED

1 To warm up, work over a single fence, then a double, then all three using only the straight route to begin with (diagram A). If you have not done any angled fences before, set the fences lower than usual or even practise going over a pole on the ground at an angle.

2 To start the exercise, approach the last fence on its own from trot (diagram B). Trot gives you more control because the horse has only one hind foot on the ground at a time.

3 When your horse understands what you want from him, start to work in a figure of eight over the first and last fences in trot, then progress to canter.

PROGRESSING

4 Ride a figure of eight over the spread (see diagram C). Make the spread narrow to start with, then gradually increase it.

5 Now you can ride all three routes: straight through the middle, a figure of eight over the uprights and a figure of eight over the spread. Vary the route to keep the horse interested and alert. Use the straight route to give him a bit of a break and encourage forward movement.

6 Remember, this is a tiring exercise, due to the number of turns, changes of rein and extra jumping effort needed to clear angled fences. Therefore, listen to your horse and stop before he makes mistakes.

How to ride it

- **Ride over the centre of each fence.**
- **Find a point on the other side of the fence** to line up with the middle of the jump. This will help you get on to the right line. Jump blocks or cones are useful for this purpose.
- **The quality of the canter is particularly important** as you are making so many turns. Remember rhythm, energy and balance. A medium-length stride is also more vital than usual as the horse is more likely to meet the fence 'wrong' off an angle. A medium-length stride is one that can be shortened or lengthened as necessary.
- **Ride purposefully.** Your horse may need some extra encouragement to jump at an angle, give him the confidence to do so.
- **Make sure you land on the correct lead.**

Fixing common faults

Running out: Approach from trot. A stop is far better than a run-out, so make the fence small enough to jump from a stand-still. Use your legs to steer, as well as your hands. Finally, check your approach: did you ask for too much angle?

Knocking down the fence: Make sure you have an even, rhythmic stride – circle to correct the canter if necessary. Are you taking off before the horse? This is easily done when jumping angles and can result in the horse hitting the jump with his front legs. Do you have enough power within the canter?

Landing on the wrong leg: Opening the new inside rein over the fence, and looking where you are going, can help to correct this. Ensure your horse is straight, between your hand and leg on the approach. That means he should be moving forwards and not leaning against either of your legs.

Poor turns: If you realize you have made a bad turn, do not approach the fence! You are schooling and therefore should help the horse as much as possible.

A SET-UP

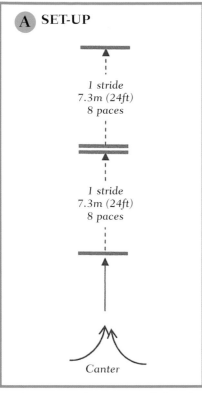

1 stride
7.3m (24ft)
8 paces

1 stride
7.3m (24ft)
8 paces

Canter

Place an upright, oxer (parallel) and upright in the centre of the arena so that they are jumpable in either direction. Ride the straight route first, on both reins.

B PROGRESSION 1

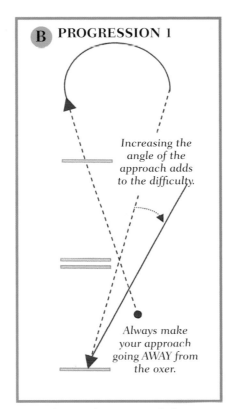

Increasing the angle of the approach adds to the difficulty.

Always make your approach going AWAY from the oxer.

Jump the uprights at an angle from trot, then canter.

C PROGRESSION 2

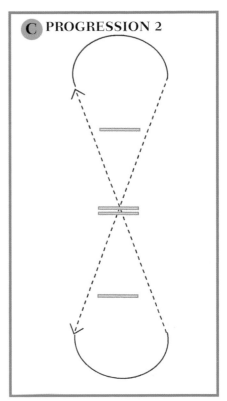

Jump the oxer at an angle.

This aerial shot shows Antoinette's horse jumping happily at a slight angle over the last part of the treble.

Left: Here the horse and rider are jumping at a very acute angle. The confidence and trust the horse appears to have in the rider comes with practice. When you start this exercise do not ask for too much angle until the horse feels confident.

Above: Here Daisy's horse is jumping confidently at an angle over the middle element of the treble.

Canter two corner fences

Uses

- To practise a cross-country fence
- For accuracy, steering and communication
- To build up trust between horse and rider

Unsuitable for

- The exercise is too advanced for a horse that has not jumped angles, or which is not able to go straight
- A horse that does not listen to his rider – this exercise can improve communication skills but cannot create them

This exercise helps you to practise tackling corner fences safely. Riding a corner correctly demands accuracy from both you and your horse, and therefore requires good communication skills. This exercise is a natural progression of the previous one. Your horse must be adept at jumping angles before you add a spread to the angle in the form of a corner.

SETTING UP

- Position both fences well off the track, half way up each long side (see diagram B). Do not use poles on the ground as the horse may confuse them with trot or canter poles and you do not want to teach him to jump those.
- Start with a small angle as in diagram A. Do not increase the angle until you can ride a straight and accurate approach and departure, over the correct part of the fence.
- Jump blocks are ideal for making corners; jump stands are suitable but can be painful if you miss your line.

GETTING STARTED

1 To warm up, work over some upright fences approached straight, then approach one or two at an angle.

2 To start the exercise, set the angle of the corner very small and the height low.

3 The line of approach is absolutely vital (see diagram A). Use arena sand or clothing to mark the front rail if you do not have coloured poles to guide you. If there is nothing in the background to line up with, mark the second rail as well. Unless you line up two points every time you jump a corner, you will forget to do it when it matters.

PROGRESSING

4 Add the second corner once you have jumped the first one a few times on both reins (diagram B).

5 At any time, if you have lost the rhythm and quality of the canter, circle. You are aiming to jump both corners from exactly the same canter – the second no faster, for example.

Left: This corner has only a very small angle and therefore can be treated like a small parallel.

(Inset) Here the horse looks quite spooky, but Darrell is staying soft and quiet and has his whip in his left hand in case the horse had tried to run out.

Top right: As the angle of the corner gets wider, the approach line has to move nearer to the point.

Right: The horse has been confident enough to stay straight. Darrell should have a whip in his right hand when jumping a corner with the apex on the right – just in case.

How to ride it

- **Pay special attention to lining** up your approach correctly.
- **Feel like you are riding down a corridor** between your hands and legs. Immediately correct any wobble on the approach.

Fixing common faults

Running out: Approach from trot and make the fence small enough to jump from a standstill. Use your legs, as well as your hands, to steer, and look ahead. Were you on the right line? Make sure your whip is in the hand nearest to the point. If he takes advantage and runs out, stop him immediately, smack him hard on his shoulder and turn him back the opposite way to which he went (turn right if he ran out to the left). Re-present him and if he jumps it well, really reward him with your voice and a pat. The whip is used on his shoulder in this case because the horse is 'going out through his shoulder' and a smack there will be more effective in explaining and correcting his error.

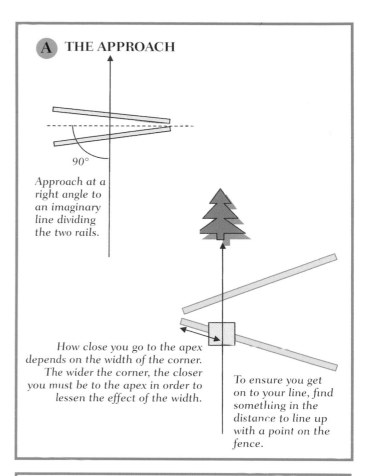

A THE APPROACH

Approach at a right angle to an imaginary line dividing the two rails.

90°

How close you go to the apex depends on the width of the corner. The wider the corner, the closer you must be to the apex in order to lessen the effect of the width.

To ensure you get on to your line, find something in the distance to line up with a point on the fence.

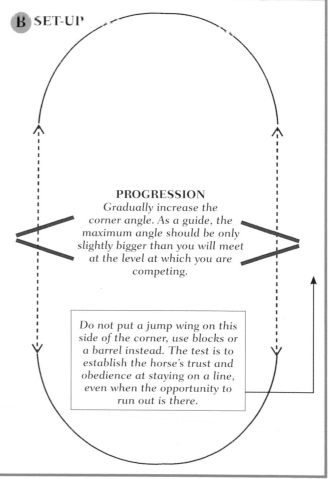

B SET-UP

PROGRESSION
Gradually increase the corner angle. As a guide, the maximum angle should be only slightly bigger than you will meet at the level at which you are competing.

Do not put a jump wing on this side of the corner, use blocks or a barrel instead. The test is to establish the horse's trust and obedience at staying on a line, even when the opportunity to run out is there.

Start with a small angle. Do not increase the angle until you can ride a straight and accurate approach and departure, over the correct part of the fence.

Leslie Law MBE

In 2004 Leslie became the first British rider to win individual Olympic gold since 1972. This tremendous achievement was the culmination of more than 15 years at top level during which he has gained two Olympic team silver medals, three European team golds and a World team bronze. At Badminton he has been in the top five four times.

Leslie's rise to the top is the result of his perseverance against the odds. To keep going, he had to sell several successful horses he had brought on from youngsters. Perhaps as a result of this, and despite being one of the most experienced riders, his Olympic gold was his first major individual title. Having secured his place in history, his success will now surely inspire generations of event riders to aim for the top.

More... www.leslielaw.co.uk

TRAINING PHILOSOPHY

■ Make sure that you have got the foundations done. You have got to take it step by step and the people you are training sometimes have to be prepared for it to deteriorate before it improves. They have to be in for the long haul. Occasionally people just want a lesson prior to a competition but that is a short-term answer. As far as training and teaching goes, the satisfaction is in putting the foundations in place and taking it step by step with a correct programme and correct preparation.

■ Producing a horse from the beginning is hugely satisfying because you can take him progressively through your own training programme. However, a schoolmaster horse can be of huge benefit to an amateur rider. If you lack time or experience, you can get more enjoyment and can learn more from a schoolmaster than from a novice that you train yourself.

■ The priority when jumping an event horse is to make sure you maintain his confidence, and I am sure that is the same for any discipline. At times, just like with people, you have to take a horse slightly out of his comfort zone to progress, but in doing so you must listen to him in order to maintain his confidence. When you are producing a young horse, you use a wide selection of jumping exercises to give him that confidence. And you provide him with a full library of experience that he can then draw on in competition. Later, when he is older and more experienced, you use exercises more as and when required.

ADVICE TO NEWCOMERS

It is important to seek professional advice and help. People are more than happy to help and the whole thing about competing is being confident. If you understand what is being asked of you then your confidence should be a lot better and then it becomes more enjoyable.

Favourite achievements

★Winning the Olympics gave me a wonderful sense of achievement. You start to think 'Wow – no British individual has won it for 32 years; all those great riders I looked up to for years and years and no one has won it since Richard Meade – here I am and I've won!'.

★ I had a great year in 2000 – the Sydney Olympics was my first real chance on the British team and H20 is such a favourite because he has done so much for me. He finished second at Badminton in the spring so it was just a really good year.

Leslie Law on Shear L'Eau at the Athens Olympics.

Introduction to the exercises

On the next few pages are some of the exercises that I regularly use.

Warm-up exercises

These exercises put the horse in the best physical and mental shape to do whatever work is planned for the main part of the session. The main priority is to warm up the muscles so that he is able to work properly, otherwise injuries can occur and weaknesses may develop. This is also the time to spot any physical problems and to gauge how horse and rider feel so that the best use is made of the time available. The warm-up should always be relevant to the work ahead and include work towards self-carriage and suppleness. Sometimes a specific preparation is required – such as lengthening and shortening before using related distances. The exercises included here are suitable for use before any show-jumping training or flatwork, or can be used as the main focus of the session. Knowing how best to warm up a particular horse takes skill and practice. Competitions can be won or lost as a result of a good or poor warm-up.

The five exercises are listed in approximate order of difficulty. Use those that you fully understand; the warm-up is not the time to experiment with new movements without help.

GETTING STARTED

1 Begin with something easy, such as walking for 10 minutes, cantering off the horse's back, or working him long and low (see photo opposite, top right).

2 The time it takes to warm up varies from about 10 minutes upwards. It is important to recognize when your horse is ready to start work. Too short a warm-up results in the horse being unable to do what you are asking because he has not loosened up sufficiently. Too long a warm-up could result in him losing interest.

PROGRESSING

3 Try to find a routine that works for your horse. The progression from the initial, easier work towards harder tasks may be seamless, or it may follow a strict pattern, such as 10 minutes of walk, followed by a halt after which he can expect to begin harder work. Be consistent; using the power of the horse's need for routine will prove particularly helpful at competitions when there is extra pressure.

4 The work should suit the horse on the day – an advanced horse may do similar exercises to a very novice one, be it in a more advanced way, if that is what he needs at that time.

5 Start using one or two of the exercises listed here and/or doing any specific preparation for the work you have planned. Some of the other exercises in this book have their own warm-up plans that can be used after or instead of those featured here.

How to ride it

- **Let the horse carry you.** You want a loose, swinging stride rather than one you are holding the horse into in a fixed manner. The more support you give the horse, the more you have to give. Do not be afraid to let go! He will not fall over if you release the rein(s) he is leaning on.
- **Ask the horse to stretch laterally,** using turns to stretch him from side to side. He must also be encouraged to stretch over his back and to track up.
- **Keep the horse within a rhythm** and work from there. Using a slightly slower rhythm allows you to use your leg more and can be helpful if the horse is reluctant to accept the leg (running away when you put your leg on).
- **The warm-up is a good time to check for any tension in your riding.** While maintaining your position, aim for a relaxed body, relaxed arms and no locking in the knee or thigh. To find the correct place for the leg, take the foot out of the stirrup and with the leather perpendicular, place the foot back in. This is a good starting point for a secure leg position. Stirrups should be two to three holes longer for warming up than for jumping. Keep a check on your personal list of usual faults.

Walk, halt, and trot transitions

Transitions improve balance, responsiveness and activity. The horse must be taught to go forwards the moment the leg is applied so he will do so instantly in front of a fence.

■ The halts must be straight. Lighten the contact as soon as the halt is established. Remain in halt long enough to find immobility. Even when halted, the horse must remain attentive so that he walks on as soon as the leg closes to ask him to move.

■ Move on into trot, and then make transitions from trot to walk, walking for just three strides before resuming trot. The same principles apply as for the halt in terms of establishing the walk and keeping the horse active. The horse must not use the hand to lean on in the downward transition.

Above: **Working long and low**
You can see here the horse is stretching – taking the bridle forward. Although it is stretching, it is not behind the vertical; it is taking its nose forwards and showing a good relaxed stride.

Giving and retaking the rein in canter

This improves balance by encouraging horse and rider to support themselves. A balanced horse is much safer to jump as he can get himself out of trouble. The exercise can help the rider to gain the confidence to rely less on the reins, enabling them to give the horse freedom over fences.

■ Give the rein forwards, 15cm (6in) up the neck, encouraging the horse to soften and drop his head a little, softening through the back. As your hand moves forwards, balance, rhythm and speed must not alter.

■ Giving the rein allows the horse more space and encourages him to move more freely. Hollowing is an indication that he is held into an outline and is simply expressing his relief that the rider has let go! Check the rider's balance does not depend on holding the reins.

Below: A good leg yield, with good crossing over, although the horse is slightly tilting his head.

Leg yield

This improves lateral suppleness, which is necessary for making good turns. It also improves response to the leg aids, which allows corrections to be made to the line of approach when jumping.

■ Start with a few steps in walk and leg yield across the diagonal. Look to where you want to go. The horse should look slightly away from the direction he is travelling in with the body parallel to the track. He must not go out through the shoulder.

■ Once you have achieved leg yield in walk, then repeat the movement in trot. You are aiming for elasticity in the rein and the horse moving freely within the pace.

■ Work towards softness – the horse may be achieving the lateral movement but in a tense way. Rather than asking anything more testing, try to get a more relaxed feel for just a step or so, and then go straight as a reward.

Leslie Law

Shoulder-in

This improves control of the shoulder and impulsion. 'Thinking' shoulder-in is useful in jumping when riding a fence off a lane, for example, to help direct the horse's attention to where you want to go.

■ Bring the shoulders off the track so that the outside fore foot traces the same line as the inside hind foot and the horse moves on three tracks. The hind legs are encouraged further underneath the horse, creating energy. The rhythm must stay the same. Do not cross your hands over the horse's neck.

Below: **Thinking shoulder-in**
A good way of approaching a fence straight out of a corner is to come through it almost thinking shoulder-in, which allows the shoulders to come out and the quarters to follow them. So, although you are not actually riding shoulder-in, you can think it and present it to the horse in that way so that you come out of the corner and approach the fence on a straight line.

A demonstration of the classic fault of just having neck bend without the shoulders moving to give enough angle; the back legs are still tracing the same track as the front legs.

A good shoulder-in: the horse is correctly on three tracks so the outside shoulder is on the same track as the inside hind leg.

Right: **Controlling the shoulder**
If the horse is inclined to fall out through the outside shoulder, use a little bit of counter bend coming through the corner to keep him straight. This is a very good example of the horse being slightly flexed to the outside to correct that outside shoulder, again in order to come out and approach the fence on a straight line.

Counter canter

This is only suitable as a warm-up for a more experienced horse as it is strenuous and requires a considerable degree of suppleness, which a more novice horse will not have achieved. It creates a better balance.

- The first step towards counter canter is to make a 2–5m (6½–16½ft) loop off the track in canter, taking care not to end up on three tracks; the hind feet should follow the same lines as the fore feet.

Inside and outside

Your inside leg is always the leg inside the bend *of the horse*. As the horse is normally bent in the same direction as the turn, this is usually the same thing, however there are exceptions:

- In canter, the horse should always be bent over the leading leg. So on a circle in counter canter, the horse is bent slightly the opposite way to the way he is turning. Therefore, on a clockwise circle your inside leg is the left leg (see diagram).
- The same applies in lateral movements, inside always means inside the horse's bend, even when he is bent away from the direction in which he is going, i.e. in leg yield.
- The aids do not change: the inside leg is used on the girth and the outside leg, behind it.

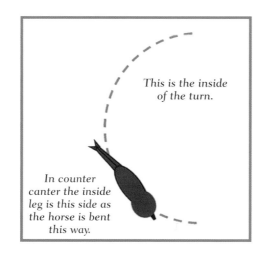

This is the inside of the turn.

In counter canter the inside leg is this side as the horse is bent this way.

Right: Here we have a good example of counter canter on a circle to the left. Good positioning, with the horse bent in the direction of the leading leg (off fore).

Halting after a fence

Uses

- Improves obedience, communication, straightness and balance

- Is calming and encourages responsiveness

Unsuitable for

- This exercise is suitable for most horses, but use it with caution for riders that are too strong with their hands, as it may make them worse

This exercise encourages obedience and straightness after landing. Straightness is essential throughout training and for avoiding problems. If you or your horse lose balance over a fence, the situation can often be rescued if the horse remains straight. Halting after a fence introduces an element of calm and additional discipline into an exercise, which is useful when dealing with an excitable horse. It also teaches riders to finish off exercises properly. It improves responsiveness to the slowing down aids and is versatile because it can be added to any exercise that works on straightness. Grids are particularly suitable for use with this exercise but halts can also be beneficial after a single fence.

SETTING UP

- Set up a fence and use jump blocks, cones, wings, a marker or the end of the arena to mark the place for the halt (see diagram A).
- Allow at least five strides space after the fence in which to halt.

GETTING STARTED

1 Warm up, and then jump without halting a few times to establish forward movement and straightness.

2 Make the first halt a comfortable distance from the last fence (five or six strides after the landing).

PROGRESSING

3 Work on the quality of the transition to halt and the halt itself. The halt must remain on the straight line after the fence. You are aiming for a smooth transition without the need for excessive rein aids. Anticipation can work in your favour with this exercise as the horse begins to expect to stop at the given point.

Fixing common faults

Resistance and lack of straightness in the halt: If the horse tries to move off, insist on the halt, then momentarily relax the rein again until you can do so without him moving, even if only for an instant. Check your own straightness; if you lean to one side over the fence or apply the aids unevenly, you cannot expect the horse to be straight. This exercise can highlight bitting or back problems; ask yourself if either could explain any difficulties you are having.

Failing to halt at the designated point: The horse must be balanced on the turn and the approach to the fence in order to be balanced after it. If he is unbalanced he will find it difficult to stop – as you would if running downhill, leaning forwards. He will also find it harder to stop if you are tipped forwards.

Restricted jumping: If the horse starts to limit the flow of his jump in anticipation of the halt, jump without halting a few times. Is your halt too close to the fence for your horse's level of training? Are you starting to halt before you land?

How to ride it

- **The priority is to establish the halt at the designated spot.** This may need firm riding at first in order to explain to the horse what is required. On landing, use half-halts to balance the horse, then, as you ask for the halt, bring your shoulders back and keep the weight in your the lower leg. Keep the elbow bent and use one firm aid to halt. When halted, lighten your seat and the rein contact. Work towards a progressively smoother transition, without tension and with minimal rein aids.

- **Do not allow the horse to lean on your hand.** If he does so, soften the rein contact then ask again. You are working towards an instant response so do not allow the slowing down process to become drawn out over several strides.

- **As soon as the horse halts,** relax the contact and relax your own body.

- **The jump must not be restricted in any way** by the fact that you are halting after it.

Spirited horses

Containing the energy

■ The aim is to keep the spirit but contain it without making a big deal out of it. Ride quietly, and work on sitting still within the movement. Moving too much or blocking movement (tensing against the horse) provokes excitability. Keep the horse listening so his mind is on the job.

■ Hot horses are also wound up by intermittent leg contact. Use a slow rhythm in trot or walk and circling in order to get your leg on the horse. Once they accept a constant contact with the leg, they gain a feeling of security and can become calmer.

■ Tense horses can also find security in repeating an exercise, especially gridwork. Grids help to regulate speed, keeping the horse in rhythm and providing a constant routine within which they can begin to relax. They also help the rider to become more consistent, which in turn helps to calm the horse.

Controlling rushing

■ There are many ways of controlling rushing. One good way is to work the horse over a fence on a circle in canter; you are coming in on a rhythm, going away on a rhythm, and are not coming from too far away on the approach. The next exercise ('Fences on a serpentine') leads on from this as a next step. A variation is to ride transitions between canter, walk and halt on the circle.

■ Rushing can be created by the rider balancing on the reins or overriding with their seat.

Rein technique

■ The crest release technique is widely used and very effective in giving the horse complete freedom to jump. It involves giving the rein forwards, on top of the horse's crest (where the mane grows) and it helps the rider to remain in balance. However, it is not suitable for all horses.

■ Onward-bound horses tend to make the highest part of the jump a little late, which can tip the front pole (diagram B). Maintaining the contact over the fence can help to correct this. By keeping a straight line between bit, hand and elbow, the rider can give the horse a sense of security and regulate the speed more effectively. Good balance is vital for this method. How firm the contact is and how much the rein is used depends on the horse.

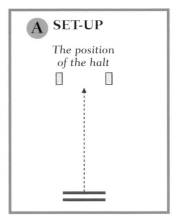

A SET-UP

The position of the halt

Mark the place to halt with jump blocks or cones, allowing at least five strides in which to halt.

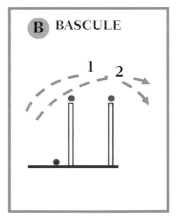

B BASCULE

The horse should make the highest point of the jump over the centre of the fence (1). If the highest point of his bascule (roundness over the fence) is too late (2), you risk knocking down the front rail.

Below: This is a very good example of the rider bringing the horse back to halt after the fence. You can see that the rider has used his upper body to get the balance and make a statement to the horse of what is required rather than going to the hand. The rider has kept a straight line between bit, hand and elbow and the horse has responded in a submissive way without resistance. The fact that the horse appears to be on a curve is due solely to the way the sequence had to be taken. The horse held a straight line throughout and back to halt.

Fences on a serpentine

Uses
- Improves turns, agility, communication, rhythm and balance

Unsuitable for
- This exercise suits most horses

This exercise improves the horse's balance, lateral suppleness and ability to turn. This is a good exercise for a spirited horse because it encourages the rider to keep their leg on, and it keeps the horse occupied. With the poles on the ground, it helps to teach riders to plan where they are going and to turn accurately. Finally, it can help to teach the horse flying changes by changing the rein over poles on the ground.

SETTING UP

- Place three equally spaced fences on the centre line at A, C and X (diagram A).
- Set the fences off the track.

GETTING STARTED

1 Warm up using turns and transitions.

2 Start by going over each fence or pole individually, then circle over two of the fences (blue line in diagram A). Start on your horse's easiest rein and make sure you work equally on both reins.

3 The quality of the work is very important; work on getting an even rhythm and a uniform bend throughout each turn. The horse must be straight while he is jumping.

PROGRESSING

4 Once you are able to maintain the rhythm and an unvarying line over two fences, make a continuous figure of eight.

5 Go large from time to time to let the horse have a break from turning.

6 When you can work consistently on the figure of eight, move the fences closer together. Space permitting, add a loop to either end as shown in diagram B. All the loops must be the same size.

How to ride it

- **Notice which loops your horse finds easier – to the right or left.** Be aware of where he falls in or out on the turns and act to prevent this the next time around.
- **Notice which way you prefer to turn** and be aware of leaning in or collapsing one way on the turns or over the fences (see photograph). Most riders are more supple on one side than the other.
- **Decide where you are going before you start** and keep looking ahead to the next fence. This helps to tell the horse the intended route.

Fixing common faults

Lack of straightness over the fences: Look ahead, so you can plan the turns. Allow the horse freedom over the fence and do not try to turn him while he is in the air.

Landing on the wrong canter lead: If the horse is reasonably balanced then continue as it is good practice for when this happens in the ring. However, over a period of time, you need to move away from coming in on the wrong lead. Firstly, teach the horse to correct the lead through a simple change, and later on, as the level of training progresses, teach him flying changes. Notice if it always happens in one particular direction. If so, check that your and your horse's balance is central. Over the fence, open the rein to whichever side you are turning (move the rein away from the neck).

Falling in or out on the turns: Balance the horse by using your inside leg and outside rein. The inside leg encourages the inside hind further underneath the horse. The outside rein provides support and prevents the horse from drifting out and bending too much to the inside (going out through the shoulder). If he leans on one of your legs, move it completely away, then use it sharply while asking for bend towards that side.

Loss of rhythm and balance: Circle without jumping to regain the canter. Make sure you are not collapsing on to the horse's shoulders on landing. It is difficult for a horse to turn if he has extra weight on his forehand. Is the horse tired? Aim to do a little well, rather than a lot badly.

A SET-UP

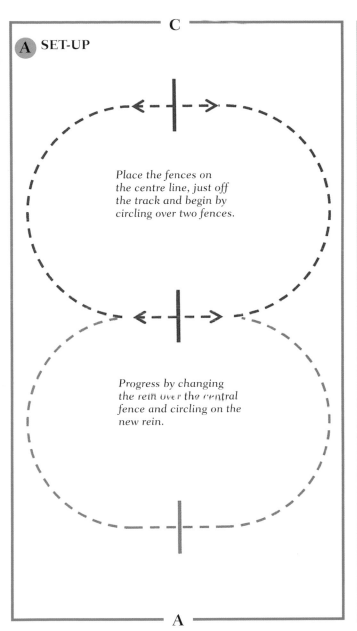

C

*Place the fences on
the centre line, just off
the track and begin by
circling over two fences.*

*Progress by changing
the rein over the central
fence and circling on the
new rein.*

A

B PROGRESSION

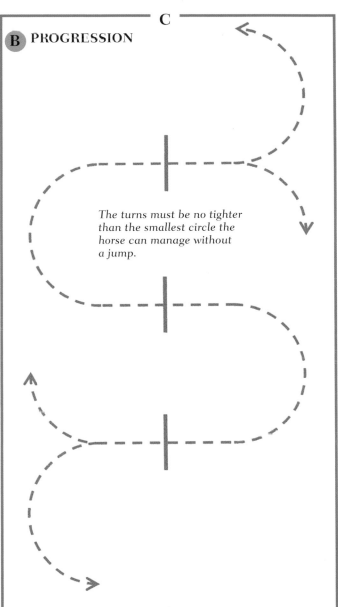

C

*The turns must be no tighter
than the smallest circle the
horse can manage without
a jump.*

A

*Move the fences closer together to create tighter turns and
extra loops.*

*A demonstration of the
classic fault of collapsing
out through the hip instead
of sitting up straight and
staying balanced in the
middle of the saddle.*

George H. Morris

Favourite achievements

★ In 1952, aged 14, I won the ASPCA Maclay and the AHSA medal finals at Madison Square Gardens. I won both these big equitation finals in the same weekend of the same year, and I am still the youngest person to win either of them.

★ In 1960 I won the Grand Prix of Aachen on Night Owl. He was a great horse. He had great heart and so much scope – though not the most careful horse in the world, over the massive solid fences at Aachen he was a real Aachen horse. In those days, Aachen was a puissance-type class with successive jump-offs – not against the clock. I think it went to five jump-offs, and they had more fences than a puissance so it was a real power test.

★ Winning an Olympic team silver medal in Rome in 1960.

★ I made a comeback in the 1980s and won the half-million dollar Du Maurier Class at Spruce Meadows in 1988. I was 50 and it was one of the biggest thrills of my life.

George Morris is chef d'équipe for the United States show-jumping team. He is widely considered to be one of the most influential trainers in the field of equestrian sports and his achievements are outstanding. Eight of his former students are Olympic medallists who between them hold team gold, team silver (twice) and individual bronze (twice). Many more of his students rank among the élite riders of the USA.

Morris conquered a childhood fear of horses to become an Olympic team silver medallist and world-renowned hunter and jumper trainer. He won the Grand Prix of Aachen, the Du Maurier Cup, team gold at the Pan American Games and eight Nations Cup team competitions. His career has thus far spanned over 50 years since he won the Hunter Seat Equitation finals aged 14. He has been training riders since he was 25.

Morris's approach to riding and teaching is detailed in three highly successful books and a recent video. Since 1978, he has been a director of the United States Equestrian Federation (formerly USET), where he is also a member of the executive and show-jumping committees.

More... www.usef.org

TRAINING PHILOSOPHY

I had a very interesting classical background in that first I was taught the principles of what we call the Forward Seat, which is a very light seat of riding. This was invented by the Italians, Caprilli and Santini, at the turn of the twentieth century and it was interpreted in every country in the world for racing. Jumping trainers interpreted it in a little different manner.

The American Cavalry School at Fort Reilly was a great exporter of the Forward Seat to other parts of our country. My American trainer, Gordon Wright, trained at Fort Reilly and taught it to me. That, coupled with classical dressage training from Bert De Nemethy, Richard Watjen and Gunnar Anderson, led me to combine the Forward Seat with the classical deep dressage seat.

To put those two seats together for jumpers is quite a tricky task: you cannot just rely on the dressage seat because that is too rigid and you cannot just rely on the Forward Seat because that is too passive. You have to put the two together – that is my philosophy of riding: to produce a very well-schooled horse, so you are in the position to do what Caprilli first taught us. That is, to use a very forward seat and *let the horse do the jumping*. It is paradoxical, but I like a very well-schooled horse under really total control but at the same time I like him to be under such control that I can teach him to help me jump the fences. To expand on that: to jump well the horse must be allowed to have complete freedom over the fence. Using the Forward Seat ensures he is unhindered as he arrives at the point of take-off and over the fence. However, this seat can only be used if the horse is schooled sufficiently well to remain under total control despite the fact that the rider is sitting very lightly. If I have taught the horse properly so that he remains under control on the approach, then he will help me by using himself in the best way when he jumps the fences.

Above: Photo courtesy of The Chronicle of the Horse/Tricia Booker.

Left: George Morris with the victorious Super League team at La Baule. From the left: Georgina Bloomberg, Laura Kraut, Beezie Madden, Schuyler Riley.

Photograph by Tina Butler.

Meredith Michaels-Beerbaum. This is an excellent picture of Meredith. She has a very classical, educated leg position – even over very big fences. Her heels are down, her ankles are flexed, her toes are out and she has got contact in her lower leg. She is one of the few Europeans who doesn't pivot on their knee and swing their legs back like windmills over the top of fences. That is because her early education in the American system created the right habits in her leg. Her seat is out of the saddle yet close to it and her back is flat. Her eyes are up and she is looking to the right – obviously she is turning that way. This horse, 'Shutterfly', has an unusual style: he jumps very long – like a steeplechase, Grand National or Maryland Hunt Cup horse; but he is very careful and very scopey, so he gets by like that. This is an excellent equitation-over-fences picture.

Many eventers find the show-jumping phase difficult. There are a number of reasons for this. Firstly, today the dressage is very exaggerated for eventing – it is almost Grand Prix dressage, which requires a very different position to that for show jumping and is very contrary to the Forward Seat. Secondly, when they go cross-country, most of them go over every fence in the safety seat, sitting back on the horse's back and often leaning on his mouth – this hinders him. This is very often against the movement and, consequently, the horse gets defensive by the third day. He is not confident that the rider won't sit back on his back and overuse their legs and perhaps even hit his mouth. So he goes to the third day defensive, which gets a hollow jumper, it gets a quick jumper, and it gets a stiff jumper. Those jumpers hit fences. Eventing really asks the horses and riders to do three very different things today, where years ago they were very similar things. That is the difficulty. Also event riders do not work on their show jumping or their show-jumping position as much as they work on the other two disciplines.

However, in my opinion, across the board the standard of riding is very good but a little bit hindering – especially the Continental school, which is exported all over the world. That is: a very deep seat and too much collection, which in turn hinders the galloping horse. I use dressage to prepare my horses for galloping and

jumping, but galloping and jumping is a different thing.

My system is built on exercises, right up to Olympic level: exercises for the rider's position, exercises for the use of aids, exercises on the flat and exercises over jumps. When I use jumping exercises, three days a week is the maximum with the very rare exception of a competition. For eventers, if they work on their cross-country one day a week, they can work on their show jumping two days, or vice versa. They will work on fitness or on their dressage for the other three or four days. In my opinion horses should not jump more than three days a week maximum.

Finally, my maxim, in any field or any endeavour, is 'the devil is in the details'. I stress that to my teams: the details of horse management, the details of veterinary care, the details of the turnout of horse and rider, the details of flatwork, the details of jumping exercises, the details of course analysis. It is all in the minute details today.

Advice for less experienced trainers: the first is to go slow and low. Slow work and low fences – don't rush and don't push over bigger fences. Repetition builds habits, and a knowledge of Classical Riding is very helpful – that, rather than 'nouveau' riding. The old, classical principles of dressage and jumping are the best.

Cayce Harrison. Cayce is at the moment of take-off to this very big oxer at Spruce Meadows. She stands this horse off at his fences a little bit because he is big and therefore needs room and time for his front end at take-off. You can see again she has a very good, very tight leg position; her lower leg is clinging to the ribs, her stirrup is placed on the ball of her foot, her heel is down and her ankle is flexed. This is a good demonstration of a seated approach, three-point contact, as used in the last two to six strides to a fence: both legs are on the horse and the seat is in the saddle making up the three points. This is versus two points of contact where you are galloping on a straight line and are slightly out of the saddle with just your two legs on the horse. Cayce's eyes are looking up and ahead and there is a very good straight line from her elbow to the horse's mouth. It's a very interesting picture because it's just at the take-off. The take-off is one of the five phases of the jump, which are: the approach, the take-off, the flight, the landing and the departure.

Photograph by Tina Butler.

ADVICE TO NEWCOMERS

Become a very rounded horse person and listen to what everybody has to say. The English riders are very rounded but their weakest link is their technical riding. Get a very good basis in horse management, a very good basis in flatwork and a very good basis in jumping work.

Introduction to the exercises

I use both of the following exercises very regularly. They are very simple, very good starters and they accommodate every horse and rider at different heights. I do them very often with every horse – of course with many different variations of distances.

Canter exercise for forward flow

George H. Morris

Uses

- For warming up

- To get a forward-going horse and improve the canter

- To help develop the rider's eye for a stride

Unsuitable for

- This exercise suits every horse and every rider

This is a great first or warm-up exercise to get the horse flowing and to work on the canter – I use it a lot. It builds confidence because the rider has to trust the horse to avoid checking him. Trotting fences is very good for horse and rider but it is just preparatory. The reality is canter work; you jump a course in canter and gallop, so that is what has to be ridden.

This exercise can also help to develop a rider's eye for a stride. The beauty of both these exercises is that they include both single fences and related fences. It is the kiss of death today for the rider when you just practise related fences. Single fences – as found out hunting – are very good for the rider's eye. People don't do enough of that today in my opinion.

The exercise can be done with a horse at any level. In January in Palm Beach I'll have 60 or 80 horses in a day, in sets of four to six, and they'll all jump the same thing. Each set is levelled: I start with the more experienced horses – for example, last year, horses such as Royal Kaliber were in the first three sets. As the day progresses, the fences get lower and horses and riders get greener, so by 3 or 4 o'clock they can be very green horses off the track.

SETTING UP

- Start with low cross rails (cross poles) and make the oxer into an open cross (see diagram B opposite page)

GETTING STARTED

1 At whatever height I start the exercise, I begin with cross rails. When I 'X' the fences I keep them the same width (see diagram B). I make them very low just to get warmed up, and then I put them up.

2 I start with long approaches that get a horse going forwards all the way to the base of the fence – to the whole distance. They go from vertical to oxer on a figure-of-eight pattern, jumping them as single fences on a slight angle. The greener the horse, the wider I make the turns and the less angled the final approach to the fences. They do the figure of eight perhaps two or three times.

3 The horse must come forwards out of the turn. He has to go forwards to the fences – that's not check, check, check, check – the rhythm must stay the same. This is about long approaches and long turns.

Daisy is going into the turn: you can see that her heel is down and her leg is impeccably placed; just in at the back of the girth. She has a flexed ankle with her toes out a shade and is showing a lovely contact in her lower leg. She is slightly out of the saddle: her hip angle is opened a little so that her seat is not too light and not too deep. That is because she is making a turn, and in order to change her weight and collect her horse, she is straightening up. She is shifting her weight back and up a little to help shift his weight back and up; she is not weighting the horse's back excessively which would restrict him. Her eyes are looking in the direction of movement and she has a very relaxed, yet elegant posture and a nice straight line from the elbow to the horse's mouth. This is a very good picture.

How to ride it

- **You have to perfect the ability to let the horse go forwards.** That is, to follow the horse to the fences then place him either to a rather deep distance so you get the right bascule, or to a balanced distance. It must never be a long, flat distance.

PROGRESSING

4 Once the work is done on the figure-of-eight, I put the horse on a straight line through the 21.3m (70ft) related distance. They work in both directions. When the fences are as low as 90cm (3ft), it is done in six strides. Then when they are bigger (1.4–1.45m/4ft 6in–4ft 9in), it is a very good discipline to do it in five. Or I mix it up – six, five, five, six – to keep the stride flexible and vary the task.

5 After that, riders can go back to a few single fences to see how that goes after doing the related distance. However, usually this is the first exercise I do when I have other things set up such as Liverpool triple bars, combinations or a course. So once I have done the single fences and the line, then I go on to something else in the ring.

Fixing common faults

Holding back: Most people are reluctant to go with a horse. They are reluctant to follow a horse to the distance – they want to check. They have to let go of him, follow him and go with him.

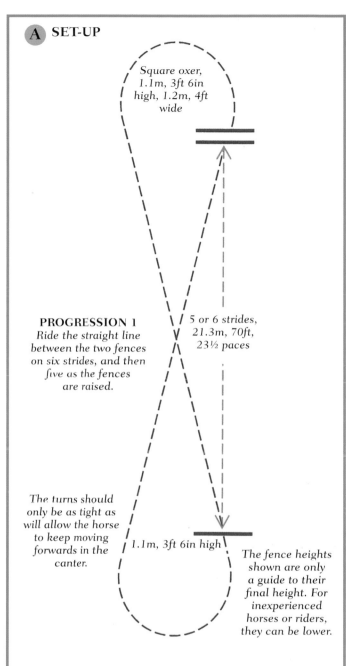

A SET-UP

Square oxer, 1.1m, 3ft 6in high, 1.2m, 4ft wide

5 or 6 strides, 21.3m, 70ft, 23½ paces

PROGRESSION 1
Ride the straight line between the two fences on six strides, and then five as the fences are raised.

The turns should only be as tight as will allow the horse to keep moving forwards in the canter.

1.1m, 3ft 6in high

The fence heights shown are only a guide to their final height. For inexperienced horses or riders, they can be lower.

Start with low cross rails and make the oxer into an open cross (see diagram B). Follow the blue route first.

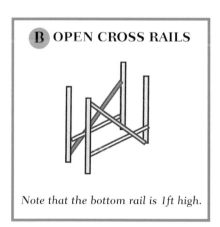

B OPEN CROSS RAILS

Note that the bottom rail is 1ft high.

Coming out of the turn, you see similar things. I'd like her stirrup a little closer to her toe, more flexion in her ankle and a deeper heel; I am very, very strict about leg position. She is going straight ahead now, so consequently she is going to lighten her seat and close her hip angle. This will put her body a little more forwards ready for the acceleration of the horse since if the horse is going straight he will go faster. The horse is alert, very well balanced and (happily) not over-flexed in his neck. His hocks are under him and it is a very compact, compressed, good quality canter stride – very nice. Here you see the compression of the canter stride, (right) you see the elongation of it.

Y-shape gymnastic for improving canter work

George H. Morris

Uses

■ Improves the canter

■ Introduces coursework

■ Makes the horse listen

■ Helps develop focus

Unsuitable for

■ This exercise suits every horse

This is a gymnastic exercise that introduces coursework and keeps the horse rideable at the canter. When you just trot gymnastics, horses become very rideable on the straight line, but once they have to canter and jump single fences off turns, they become fresher and stronger – because they are cantering. A gymnastic is a rat-trap in a sense: you trot in and it does the work. This exercise has a little addition at the end that asks for control and obedience in the canter. This part of the exercise is the more difficult – the horse has to listen, especially to the half-halt, and that is where the canter work comes in. He has to stay in the corners – not cut them, he has to steer at the gallop, he has to listen to the half-halt, he has to listen to the inside leg, he has to listen to the outside leg. This makes the horse more responsive to the aids and develops the rider's ability to keep their focus through quite a few jumping efforts and turns.

SETTING UP

■ Place the fences in the pattern shown (diagram A) but with all of them set as cross rails (cross poles). The oxers start off as open crosses (see previous exercise, diagram B, p.107).

■ For inexperienced horses or riders, build the grid slowly, one fence at a time.

■ The two fences after the grid point towards the corners of the arena. The size of arena determines the distance between them – it may be four to seven strides, or even three in a tight arena.

■ The fence heights shown are only a guide to their final height. For a very green horse the fences could be 76cm (2ft 6in). For an open jumper they could be 1.4m (4ft 6in).

GETTING STARTED

1 I start with a series of cross rails, some with a spread, and I make the approach to the fences in the corners easy (see the route marked on diagram A). This last part of the exercise can be added later for less experienced horses and riders.

2 If the horse is so green that a line of fences is too much at first, then I start with a cross pole and take all the other fences out. Then I put up the front of the oxer, and then the back of it so it builds rail by rail. That is, of course, much more time-consuming, but for a very green or screwed-up horse, it is the way to do it. That is the way Bert de Nemethy always did it: he took all the fences out but the first, then he added the second and the third and so on.

3 The second or third time I will raise just the second fence (2) and possibly the last fence (4) of the grid. Everything I do is very progressive: I start low and simple and then become higher, wider, and more difficult. I square the oxers 95 per cent of the time for all exercises to encourage a good bascule.

PROGRESSING

4 Raise the last two fences of the grid (3 and 4), see diagram. When raising the oxer, spread it by moving the back rail further out.

5 Vary the route taken for the two fences in the corners (diagram B). Approach them from either direction and jump them straight or at an angle. Approach the oxer off a short half turn, or the vertical off a sharp left turn, or reverse it. You can have a long approach to either fence – there is a lot that can be done with those two fences.

Georgina Bloomberg. This is an interesting turn. Georgina is looking up and ahead and her position is impeccable for galloping and jumping horses. Notice how she is using her eyes. You can see that it is not very important that a horse is flexed or over-flexed for galloping and jumping; he needs his neck to balance himself and in gesturing for that, this horse's head is up and that's where it should be. He is on his hocks: they are underneath him and he is sitting in this turn – he is a beautifully balanced horse.

Photograph by Tina Butler.

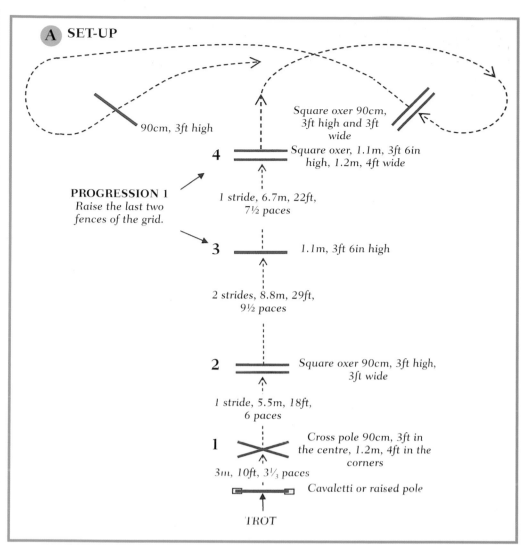

A SET-UP

Left: Begin with all the fences set as cross rails; the oxers start off as open cross rails (cross poles).

90cm, 3ft high

Square oxer 90cm, 3ft high and 3ft wide

4 Square oxer, 1.1m, 3ft 6in high, 1.2m, 4ft wide

PROGRESSION 1
Raise the last two fences of the grid.

1 stride, 6.7m, 22ft, 7½ paces

3 1.1m, 3ft 6in high

2 strides, 8.8m, 29ft, 9½ paces

2 Square oxer 90cm, 3ft high, 3ft wide

1 stride, 5.5m, 18ft, 6 paces

1 Cross pole 90cm, 3ft in the centre, 1.2m, 4ft in the corners

3m, 10ft, 3⅓ paces

Cavaletti or raised pole

TROT

Below: PROGRESSION 2 Many different routes may be taken over the two fences in the corners to add variety and get the horse very soft in the turning. These are just some examples, with the more difficult routes shown in brown.

How to ride it

- **Have sufficient impulsion for the cavaletti** – the horse has to be active and lively but not too fast. If he is too fast he will mess up the distance from the cavaletti to the cross rails. Through the gymnastic, regulate the impulsion through your hands and keep the horse on a straight centre line with your hands and legs.
- **The distances are all tight.** That 8.8m (29ft) after the first oxer (2) is a very short distance – sometimes I make it 8.5m (28ft) from the cross rail to the first oxer. This means the horse has got to listen to the half-halt – he has to listen to the hands. After that first little oxer he *definitely* has to listen to the half-halt, because he could easily do one stride but he must do two. If he is too quick and getting too deep to the vertical then pull up after the little oxer. But do that when the fences are still cross rails. It is a very common mistake to put the fences up instead of insisting that the horse obeys the half-halt.

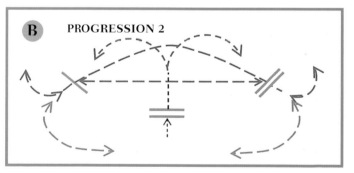

B PROGRESSION 2

Fixing common faults

Hesitation: With a very green horse, a very green rider or a stopper, hesitation to the exercise is a common fault. With the hesitant horse you have the stick and a spur so you teach them about your legs through using these.

Too quick through the exercise: This is more common with older horses and made horses. They get too fast through the exercise – that is where you have to pull them up.

Drifting to the side – not holding a straight line: You have to keep them on a straight line with an opening rein.

Matt Ryan OAM

Favourite achievements

★ *Going to the Seoul Olympics as reserve and seeing the quality of the European-based opposition made me make up my mind to base myself in the UK – and that was a pretty big commitment, I had been a working pupil for Richard Meade and had originally thought I would need to be in the UK for two or three years – but this is my 16th year!*

★ *People started to notice me when I rode Kibah Tic Toc around Badminton in 1992. It was such a difficult cross-country course and we really shone so that was pretty special and basically got me my slot in the Australian Olympic team for Barcelona.*

★ *Winning two gold medals in Barcelona was spectacular! People saw me at Badminton, then at Barcelona they realized I might not be a flash in the pan – so that was pretty amazing.*

Continued...

Matt Ryan is a triple Olympic gold medallist with one individual and two team gold medals. He was a member of the victorious Australian team at the Barcelona, Atlanta and Sydney Olympic Games but was forced to retire at Atlanta due to an injury to his horse. At Barcelona, he won his individual gold medal on Kibah Tic Toc, half-brother to Kibah Sandstone, the horse he rode to team gold in Sydney.

Since Matt came to the UK in 1989, he has achieved frequent top ten placings at CCI three- and four-star level, and has been in the top ten four times at Burghley and three times at Badminton, where he was second in 1995. He is consistently ranked among the top fifteen event riders in the world. Matt is married to Marie and is based in Wales.

More... www.mattryan.co.uk

ADVICE TO NEWCOMERS

Having a very good secure, safe position is incredibly important. However, to reach the very top, you have also got to be dedicated to educating yourself and your horse on the flat. The people who win the major events these days are those who get their noses in front after the dressage – and they're very hard to catch then!

TRAINING PHILOSOPHY

I have had some major influences in my life. Obviously, my family are among the most important to me; my parents encouraged my brothers and myself to reach the very top. They inspired us to think of Olympics and to enjoy riding. They supported me with their belief that I could get to dizzy heights. People are often scared to do that because they think if they tell you that you are going to hold an Olympic gold medal, it's most likely that you will fail. But someone's got to do it! So my parents were an amazing support for me.

As far as technicalities go, as I was growing up, Lucinda Prior-Palmer (Green) was beating the rest of the world with her style of cross-country riding. She was one of my idols and her position has had a strong influence on my style of riding. Another influence was Vicky Roycroft. Leading up to the Barcelona Olympics, Kibah Tic Toc was having lots of show jumps down; Vicky spent a lot of time with us in the Australian training camp. She also helped me mentally by giving me some basic philosophy in show jumping, which I have taken with me ever since.

My brother Heath was a major influence on me when I was a teenager. He spent time training me in Austria and Germany and convinced me to remain very competitive in the dressage. I truly believe that the control we learn in schooling horses on the flat definitely helps our precision – particularly nowadays where accuracy is so important for eventing. Hence, flatwork is a very important part of my training.

Matt Ryan

Favourite achievements

★ *Winning the team gold medal in front of my home crowd was something I'll never forget. My career was in the doldrums to a degree leading up to Sydney but my personal circumstances had changed a lot so my motivation and outlook on life was much more positive. You would have thought that winning an individual gold medal should have meant more than winning a team gold but, funnily enough, winning that team gold at home certainly outweighed the emotions and euphoria that followed Barcelona.*

TRAINING PEOPLE

One of the main things I find people lack an understanding about on the flat is how to get horses on the bit, and what 'on the bit' means. They struggle with the concept of real roundness and unfortunately interpret it as a shape, not as a feeling of what the horse is doing through his body. If I am teaching and people don't have enough control when it comes to jumping and cross-country, I will say, 'Listen, get your flatwork in order and you will be able to do this exercise.' If you can't shorten up, can't lengthen, or can't control your horse on turns or whatever it may be, that has a lot to do with a lack of control in your flatwork.

When I am teaching jumping, I prioritize position most of the time; keeping the lower leg forwards, not allowing the upper body to fall too far forwards and letting the horse have lots of rein. I also work on getting a proper canter stride. I encourage people to keep travelling forwards on a 12-foot stride not just for cross-country but for show jumping as well. We have to get close to a fence and find that deep spot by moving up to it, not shortening. We have to see a stride without having to shorten to look for it. This is a very difficult concept for many people – they prefer to shorten up to look for those spots and they get used to doing that. As a result, they are not travelling at the correct pace, so they struggle with getting the correct number of strides into related distances and combinations. As far as seeing a stride goes, it is very important to be able to do that if you want to reach the top and be successful there. It is very difficult to do, very difficult to train, but yes, trainable and you can do it. People have to work on related distances to get the feel of seeing a stride. If you can't see a stride, at the end of the day, you will not get to the top.

TRAINING HORSES

My priority in training horses to jump is to get them to use themselves as much as possible. To achieve that, I work on exercises to encourage them to jump up steeper and have a higher parabola. The old classic eventing formula of being fast and flat over fences is not what we encourage now, even for the actual cross-country. There are safety issues; I want my horses sharp, I want them getting closer, getting deeper to fences so they work harder. As eventers, we quite often get frightened of getting close to the fences, so a big aspect of show-jump training is doing that often enough, consistently enough that our horses memorize the sequence of the jump required. This is called muscle memory reflex, which is a term used by all sports people these days. Quite often grids are the only way to achieve that. This is particularly so when you are working with younger horses whose adjustability is not as good as you would like it to be. You rely on related distances or grids to make sure that they meet the more difficult fences at an accurate spot.

FITNESS

Fitness is also very important to me, and one way my programme differs from other people's is that I do not believe in doing roadwork for four to six weeks to harden horse's legs up. I am totally against that. I try to stay off the roads and keep my horses on as good a surface as I possibly can to avoid concussion problems. Pure athletes have as much cushioning as they possibly can in their trainers to prevent wear and tear on their joints and limbs. It is the same for horses: the more time they spend pounding on the ground the more damage you are doing. The concept of hardening the legs is some sort of old wives' tale. You don't harden their legs. You tone them up. So I am steady with my horses in the first week; I might do a little light hacking down the road for half an hour or put them on the horse walker. After that, I start schooling them in the arena so all the trot and canter work is done on good surfaces to preserve their soundness and longevity. I believe I can tone up my horses so much better doing dressage than I can out on a hack. On top of that,

I am educating the horse and this harks back to my grounding in prioritizing flatwork. The only thing that flatwork can't achieve is cardio-vascular fitness, so obviously I have to do gallop work; I no longer do this on the flat though, I try to work on the hills. However, all the canter work – the basic training of the canter and canter muscling – is done on the flat. These days you don't spend ten or fifteen minutes doing slow canters as the main part of your fitness programme.

The most important thing as far as getting the horses fit cardio-vascularly is getting the horse's heart rate up. It is pretty well accepted that you need be able to push a horse way up to about 200 beats a minute for no more than 30 seconds or so. You want to achieve that with the *least stress possible*, meaning that you don't have to go *fast*; you want to get the horses pulling up a hill. The more times you go fast, the more wear and tear you provoke. If you can't feel or see how hard you are pushing your horses, then you have to get hold of a heart monitor. The horses do have to learn to be pretty quick, but hills rather than speed should do the work. It is a form of interval training with the intervals dictated by how long the hill is. You have to get back down the bottom as quickly as you can. Don't let the horse recover too quickly. If you are in any doubt about fitness work, consult your trainer or vet.

When getting a horse to peak fitness I would definitely gallop on every third, rather than fourth day because as long as you are not doing any damage, the harder you work them the fitter they will get. Galloping every three days will only be in the last month leading up to a three-day event. From the beginning, three months out, it might only be once every five days but it will gradually be beefed up.

On top of that, every time a horse has done any sort of canter work, we use ice boots. I think that the eventing world in general is really backward in picking up on aggressive cooling of horses. If you run competitively, horses get hot and need aggressive cooling. Luckily, in Australia because of the heat, we are very aware of it. I am sure that awareness has contributed to our success worldwide, despite our lack of numbers.

Apart from technique and fitness, it is also important to keep the work interesting and relevant. I often vary the exercises I do and let my imagination run – what did I see at the last event? What caused a bit of trouble? I try not to let myself get set on just one or two things. Some places have movable jumps so you can ask them to set up something specific like a jump into water or in water. Look at what is around on cross-country courses so you are always sufficiently prepared.

Introduction to the exercises

My general philosophy for these exercises was to look at what we need to learn jumping-wise so we can cope with the modern style of cross-country courses. Hence there are angles, narrow fences and related distances on sometimes bending lines because this is what is happening in the cross-country these days.

Straight lines: grid to arrowhead

Uses

■ Improves straightness, accuracy, focus and feel

Unsuitable for

■ Horses and riders that have very little jumping experience

It is important to introduce the horse to meeting arrowheads after other fences on a related distance. In competition, he must remain accurate and straight, no matter what has happened over the preceding fences in a combination. This exercise is the first of a series of four that develop this skill. The cross poles get the horse jumping the centre of the fence, then the first vertical sets him up to meet the parallel on a perfect stride. The parallel encourages a good round jump two strides before the narrow fence. It is more difficult to be accurate after any spread fence because it takes more energy to jump them and that can cause the horse to speed up or to shift his weight on to his forehand. This is an excellent exercise for improving control and encouraging the rider to sit up. However, it is advisable for horse and rider to have seen some form of easy arrowhead beforehand.

SETTING UP

■ Place the grid in the centre of the working area to allow work on both reins (diagram A).
■ Start with two cross poles, then add a third.

GETTING STARTED

1 If you have not done arrowheads for a while, warm up over the one shown, which is suitable for any level of horse. It is particularly good for the rider as the horse may spook at the block, testing the rider's skill at keeping him straight.

2 Start the exercise by riding a simple grid of cross poles to encourage straightness (diagram A). Progress only when the horse stays straight, in a good rhythm. Make sure the distance is comfortable for your horse. The last two strides are fairly short because it is best if the horse is close to the arrowhead at the point of take-off. The closer he is, the less likely he is to run out as the fence fills more of his vision.

PROGRESSING

3 Add an arrowhead at the end of the grid (diagram A). With a novice horse, start with a full width fence with sloping rails. Otherwise, use short poles to create a narrow fence. Keep the height low until you can do the exercise well.

4 Change the third element into a spread by adding a back rail, no lower than the centre of the cross. This will make the arrowhead slightly more difficult, so ride through the grid a couple of times before progressing further.

5 Raise the second and third fences. Make sure you remain straight as the crosses are no longer there to help you. Make the parallel low at first.

6 Next, take the sloping rails away from the arrowhead. This fence does not need to be more than 84cm (2ft 9in) because if everything goes wrong over the parallel, the horse should still jump the arrowhead.

7 Gradually raise the vertical and oxer up to 1.1m (3ft 6in) maximum. The arrowhead can be varied (see 'Variations').

VARIATIONS ON THE ARROWHEAD

ARMS SLOPING AWAY (centre photo)
Horses can find this fence confusing – particularly when it forms part of a combination. Practise small variations of it on its own before including it in the grid.

MORE IMPOSING
Use a filler or something spooky to vary the exercise for the horse and encourage him to respect the fence; short poles are light and fall easily. A spooky fence will improve the rider, as they will have to work harder to keep the horse straight.

NARROWER
This is good for both horse and rider. It is possible to make the arrowhead narrower when it is at the end of a grid than when it is ridden as an individual fence. This is because the grid sets the horse up.

In the series shown opposite:
Left: When it comes to doing any type of related lines particularly gridwork, your line becomes very important. You can see Daisy is very focused on the last arrowhead, which is initially set so that the rails act as wings directing the horse right into the middle of it. To make it easier and encourage a horse to stay even straighter, those rails could be put up on blocks instead of having them sloping down to the ground.

Centre: Now Daisy is up to her third rail and has stayed very straight down the grid, which is excellent. The horse has pricked his ears, so he is now locked on to the final element. That is why we try to establish these lines as early as we can: so the horse has time to assess the jump. You can see the wings here are no longer going down to encourage the horse into the fence; they are actually angled back, away from you to accentuate the arrowhead. If we wanted to make this a little more difficult, then instead of having the ends of the poles up on blocks, you could slope them down.

How to ride it

- **The approach must be straight**, with enough impulsion (energy).
- **Sit up between each element** and work to keep the horse together with the leg around him and an even rein contact.
- **Sit still** so that you are able to feel any loss of straightness through your legs, seat, back and hands in time to deal with it.
- **Everything must happen smoothly** and your focus must be on straightness.

Fixing common faults

Hitting the arrowhead: If the horse repeatedly hits it despite having a good quality canter on the approach, then make the fence more imposing: see 'Variations'. If he is going too fast, remove the arrowhead and halt after the oxer. Are you sitting still?

Running out: This is the worst fault. Try to make your effort in keeping your horse straight, firm enough that he finds it uncomfortable; don't let him learn that run-offs are an easy option. Go back a stage.

Refusal at the arrowhead: Did you over-restrict the horse on the approach? Did he over-jump the parallel and arrive unbalanced on a poor stride?

Problems at the parallel: The parallel will highlight any problems with flattening (front rail down), restriction (back rail down) or the rider in front of the movement (front rail down). All these things will affect the approach to the arrowhead. Remove the arrowhead until they are resolved.

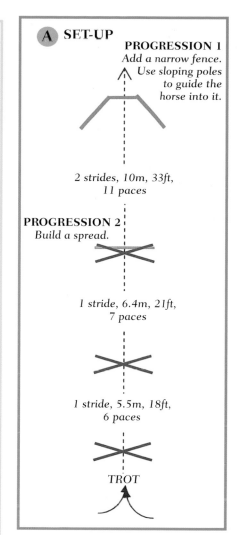

A SET-UP

PROGRESSION 1
Add a narrow fence. Use sloping poles to guide the horse into it.

2 strides, 10m, 33ft, 11 paces

PROGRESSION 2
Build a spread.

1 stride, 6.4m, 21ft, 7 paces

1 stride, 5.5m, 18ft, 6 paces

TROT

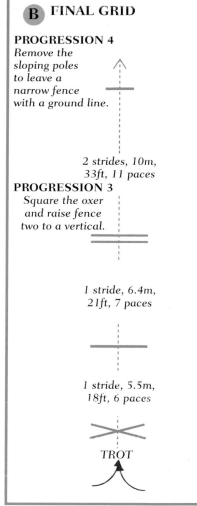

B FINAL GRID

PROGRESSION 4
Remove the sloping poles to leave a narrow fence with a ground line.

2 strides, 10m, 33ft, 11 paces

PROGRESSION 3
Square the oxer and raise fence two to a vertical.

1 stride, 6.4m, 21ft, 7 paces

1 stride, 5.5m, 18ft, 6 paces

TROT

Place the grid in the centre of the arena to allow work on both reins. Start with two cross poles, then add a third.

WARM-UP FENCE
This fence is optional. Use a jump block, set very low, as the apex of the arrowhead and set the arms of the fence at a wide angle.

Jump the routes 1 and 2 in the order shown, at trot. If the horse refuses do not turn away – it can be jumped from a standstill. This fence is not suitable for including in the grid as it is too narrow and too low in relation to the other fences.

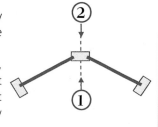

Right: The final shot shows Daisy completing the grid and the horse is dead straight down the middle of the arrowhead. Even when you're jumping a last element, you must always imagine there is yet another arrowhead to follow, one or two strides away. Daisy is looking straight ahead at that imaginary next fence. We have progressed a bit so the arrowhead doesn't have any wings whatsoever. That looks like a good job.

Matt Ryan

Straight lines to related angles and arrowheads

Uses

■ Improves straightness, accuracy, turns, focus and obedience

Unsuitable for

■ Horses that have not already done easier arrowheads and angles

This exercise improves straightness over narrow fences and angles at related distances. It develops accuracy and encourages the horse and rider to focus. It is the next stage on from the previous exercise as it is more difficult to keep the horse straight without the help of the grid.

SETTING UP

■ Start with small fences in the middle of the arena (see diagram A).
■ Place ground lines on each side of them so they can be jumped from either direction.

GETTING STARTED

1 Warm up by riding the vertical and oxer individually on both reins. If it is some time since you last did them, warm up over easy arrowheads.

2 Start the exercise by making easy turns between the fences (route 1, diagram A). Ride the vertical and parallel straight and then at an angle. Concentrate on the quality of the canter with the horse going forwards in a good rhythm. Return to this stage at any point in the exercise to regain a good canter if the quality is lost.

PROGRESSING

3 Ride the related distances in the order shown in diagram B (routes 2 and 3). Initially, ride the parallel after the vertical so that the horse meets it on a perfect stride.

4 Then ride the arrowhead to the vertical and vice versa (routes 4 and 5). Do not raise the fences at this stage. They should be at a height that is easy for you and your horse, and no higher than 90cm (3ft). Turn far enough away from the fences to get absolutely straight for them. Stay straight for several strides on landing.

5 Link the fences in a simple course (route 6, diagram C). There must be no loss of straightness or accuracy due to the turns. Concentrate on remaining focused and getting on to a good line.

6 Ride some tighter turns, as shown in diagram D.

7 Raise the fences to no higher than 1m (3ft 3in) and ride your own course. The rhythm must remain constant and the stride must stay round.

How to ride it

■ **Keep the rhythm and forward momentum** with the horse travelling at the required stride length for the related distance. A 3.7m (12ft) stride is normal. Don't hold too much; you can end up over-restricting the horse as you strive for precision. Control him with a light rein and the leg in constant contact, without clamping it around his sides.

■ **Establish straightness** as far away from the fence as possible by making sharper turns, but not so sharp that you lose forwardness. The earlier you get on to a straight line, the more time you have to make any corrections. A broader turn would bring you on to that straight line later and give the horse more opportunity to drift out through his shoulder.

■ **Circle if you lose canter quality or make a poor turn.** However, I would only circle if you are far enough away from the jump so as not to confuse the horse. Do not pull off a fence at a late stage; we do not want the horse to consider a run off is ever allowed.

Fixing common faults

Run-outs: Refer to the previous exercise. Make sure he has time to see the fences and approaches them straight.

Refusals: Make sure that you do not over-restrict the horse with your hands. The straightness comes from the horse going forwards from the leg. It is almost impossible to keep a horse straight if he is not going forwards.

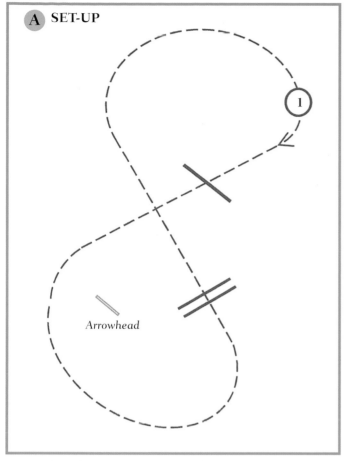

A SET-UP

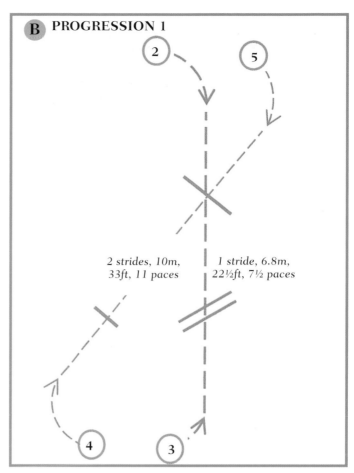

B PROGRESSION 1

2 strides, 10m, 33ft, 11 paces

1 stride, 6.8m, 22½ft, 7½ paces

Arrowhead

Start with small fences in the middle of the arena, with ground lines on either side. Ride the vertical and the oxer on both reins (route 1).

Ride the double of angles and the arrowhead both ways. Go large around the arena and circle before approaching the fences.

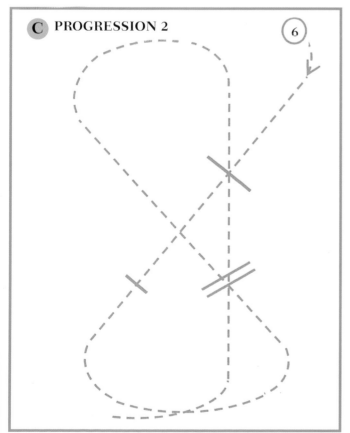

C PROGRESSION 2

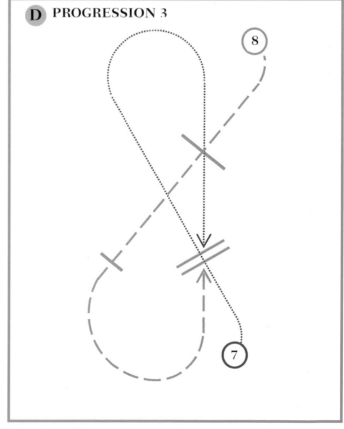

D PROGRESSION 3

Ride a simple course (route 6), first in the direction shown, then in the opposite direction.

Ride more difficult turns, then raise the fences. Add fillers to make some of the fences more interesting.

Matt Ryan

Matt Ryan

Uses

- For accuracy, turning, steering, obedience and focus

- It improves the partnership between horse and rider

Unsuitable for

- This exercise is only for reasonably experienced combinations that are already jumping narrow fences and corners confidently and accurately

Combinations on a curve are increasingly commonplace in eventing so it is essential to practise them. This exercise demands a high level of accuracy, communication and focus and so helps to build the partnership between horse and rider. It improves the rider's ability to use the outside aids on a turn and to prevent any loss of straightness before it occurs. The related distance encourages the rider to keep the rhythm, sit still and keep coming forwards to the fences.

This exercise is a progression of the previous one.

SETTING UP

- This exercise is best done in a field due to the space required.
- Build a small corner halfway up the side of the working area.
- Make the curve no tighter than that of a 30–40m (98½– 130ft) circle.
- Add a vertical three or four strides away on a gentle curve.

GETTING STARTED

1 Warm up over some angled fences, and then ride a single corner (see pp. 90–91, for more information on how to approach a corner). Work on both reins.

2 Develop the exercise in stages, starting with a corner to a vertical (diagram A).

3 Vary the route, as shown in red, to keep the horse listening and interested.

4 Break up the work by going large in medium canter or riding one or two fences straight instead of on a curve.

PROGRESSING

5 Replace the vertical with another corner (diagram B). Approach the first one on a straight line as shown.

6 In preparation for adding the third fence (diagram C), ride through jump stands where it will be placed.

7 After the exercise, jump some easier fences on a straight line to finish.

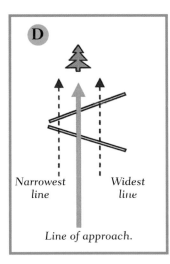

Narrowest line   *Widest line*

Line of approach.

Line of approach and the widest line it is safe to take.

THE LINE OVER A CORNER

- Find the widest and narrowest parts of the corner that you could safely jump and take a line halfway between them (D). This means you jump a wider part of the fence than you need to, but you significantly reduce the risk of running out.

- Sometimes a tree or other object is placed inside the corner (E), to prevent riders taking a line that is too wide. This can be exploited by riding as close as possible to that object. Again, the extra effort is outweighed by the reduced risk of a run-out.

- All corners must be jumped straight, even when they are on a curve.

Right: The horse is on a nice flowing stride throughout this sequence. On landing over the first corner, the rider has already started to turn him. The horse is not resisting and is looking towards the next element. The rider has judged the turn well so she has arrived in the middle of the second jump.

A SET-UP

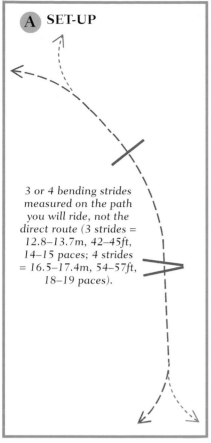

3 or 4 bending strides
measured on the path
you will ride, not the
direct route (3 strides =
12.8–13.7m, 42–45ft,
14–15 paces; 4 strides
= 16.5–17.4m, 54–57ft,
18–19 paces).

Place a small corner halfway up the
working area. Jump the corner on both
reins, then add the vertical. Ride the
corner to the vertical first then vice versa.

B PROGRESSION 1

3 or 4 bending strides

Replace the vertical with another small
corner, keeping the distance the same.

C PROGRESSION 2

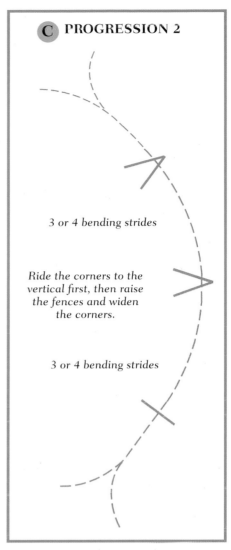

3 or 4 bending strides

Ride the corners to the
vertical first, then raise
the fences and widen
the corners.

3 or 4 bending strides

Add a vertical three or four strides before
the two corners.

How to ride it

- **Keep riding forwards to the fences** – the strides between them must all be the same length.
- **The horse must stay straight in the air** over all the fences. If you turn too quickly or restrict his landing over the corners, he will catch the back pole. Cross-country, either of these faults could cause a fall.
- **The horse must remain central between** your hand and leg – do not allow him to lean on to your outside leg or rein. The turns must be soft so the whole exercise flows smoothly.
- **Look where you are going!**

Fixing common faults

Drifting to the outside: This exercise is not designed to sort out problems with basic straightness. That has to be achieved firstly on the flat and then by using grids on a straight line. Keep control of the shoulder by using the outside rein and leg. Riding the route marked in red (diagram A) may also help to control the shoulder.

Advanced accuracy within a course

Uses

- Improves accuracy, turning, steering, obedience, focus and the partnership between horse and rider

Unsuitable for

- This exercise is only for reasonably experienced combinations that are already jumping narrow fences and corners

This exercise puts arrowheads, angles and turns into context, as you might find them in a cross-country course. The more familiar the horse is with the sort of questions he will face at an event, the more confident he becomes. Using show jumps gives you control over the situation because you can tailor the fences to suit your horse's stage of training.

The aim is to stay in a constant rhythm, with good balance and a sense of flow, despite jumping fences that are narrow or spooky or off a turn. All the fences and turns must be ridden smoothly, with precision, which requires concentration and obedience. The short turns and spooky fences really help to sharpen the reflexes of both horse and rider; the combination of spreads and narrows improves the ability to adjust the stride quickly. Because this exercise is mentally and physically testing, it helps both of them learn to remain focused.

This exercise is a progression of the previous ones in this section: horse and rider must have jumped arrowheads, spooky fences and angles recently.

SETTING UP

- Set up the course and use ground lines so that all fences can be jumped from both directions.
- Begin over the vertical and oxer, jumping them at a slight angle to avoid the other fences.
- Then progress in the order shown.

GETTING STARTED

1 Warm up by circling around the fences, making transitions, lengthening and shortening. The horse must be responsive to your aids and working in a good, round, forward-going canter. Do not start the exercise until a good quality canter is established. Return to this stage at any time.

2 Start by jumping the vertical and oxer on easy lines to set the pace and establish a good rhythm.

3 Then jump one of the arrowheads and the water tray on their own off a straight line so that those fences are introduced before being added to a combination.

PROGRESSING

4 Work on straightness by riding the direct combinations: arrowhead to vertical, water tray to parallel. Then ride the angled combination of the vertical and water tray, both ways.

5 Ride the combinations on or from curving lines: arrowhead 2 to the water tray, the two arrowheads, arrowhead 1 to the parallel.

6 Finally, ride your own course, working on staying in a constant rhythm with even-length strides between all the fences. The arrowheads can be made as easy or imposing as you like (see 'Variations', p. 114).

7 As the exercise is quite demanding, you could finish with a spread on a straight line to help the horse mentally unwind. Ride this off a more open, but not flat, stride.

This is obviously part of a combination – a curved line of narrow fences. As I've jumped the stump, feeling very secure that I have got over the fence, I've looked at the next element and also indicated to the horse by opening my rein to the left. You have always got to be a little careful in taking up too much contact over the fence because sometimes the horses can get a little offended and lose the quality and roundness of the jump. Hopefully the more schooled they become, as long as the rider is tactful, then they can indicate to the horse the direction they are going, without being offensive.

How to ride it

■ **Use the straight-line related distances** to help establish rhythm and an even length of stride.

■ **The more precise the task, the more still you must sit.** It is fine to end up in an ugly position sometimes, so long as you let the horse do his job and do not give him confusing signals by moving unnecessarily. If you have to continually pull and push, the exercise is probably too advanced for your current stage of training.

■ **Stay calm and focused** so you communicate this to your horse.

■ **The stride must stay round,** do not allow it to become stilted, particularly between the arrowheads.

■ **Be clear about where you are going** – open the rein if necessary and look for the next fence.

■ **Take a break from time to time** and do something easy or let the horse walk and stretch. This exercise is as mentally intense for horse and rider as it is physically demanding for the horse.

Fixing common faults

Run-outs: Refer to 'Straight lines: grid to arrowhead', pp. 114–115. Question yourself about the cause, and go back a stage if you are unsure of the reason. Make sure you are riding at the right pace to make the related distances work.

Lack of control: This exercise can show up any problems with bitting, martingales, backs or joints. Find the cause of the trouble and in the meantime take the work back a stage or two so that you can finish on a good note. Don't be afraid to make changes to bits or tack – just keep the task relatively simple until you find something that works.

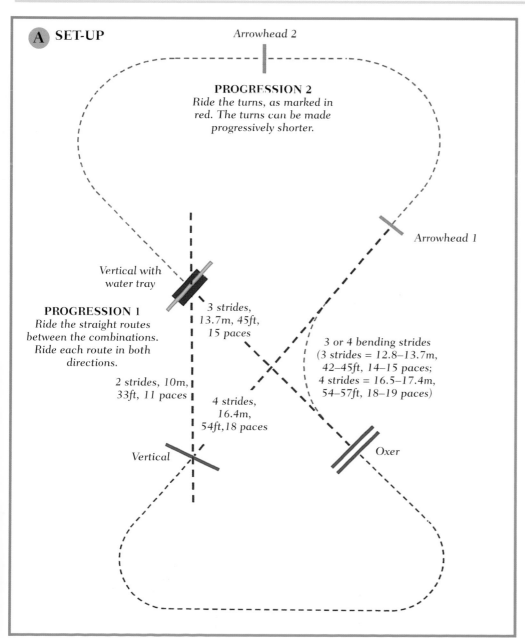

A SET-UP

Arrowhead 2

PROGRESSION 2
Ride the turns, as marked in red. The turns can be made progressively shorter.

Arrowhead 1

Vertical with water tray

PROGRESSION 1
Ride the straight routes between the combinations. Ride each route in both directions.

3 strides, 13.7m, 45ft, 15 paces

3 or 4 bending strides (3 strides = 12.8–13.7m, 42–45ft, 14–15 paces; 4 strides = 16.5–17.4m, 54–57ft, 18–19 paces)

2 strides, 10m, 33ft, 11 paces

4 strides, 16.4m, 54ft, 18 paces

Oxer

Vertical

Set up the course and use ground lines so that all fences can be jumped from both directions. Begin over the vertical and oxer, jumping them at a slight angle to avoid the other fences. Then progress in the order shown.

Gill Watson FBHS

Favourite achievements

★*Winning Burghley was unexpected, and my first major success. Looking back, I think it opened up new horizons and gave me an insight into how much there was to learn in the sport. I now get huge pleasure in watching teams not only win, but develop their individual talents.*

The gold medal-winning Young Rider team at the European Championships in Portugal 2005, (left to right) Alex Postolowsky, Oliver Smith, Gill Watson, Lucy Holliday, Isobel Taylor.

Photo by Alex Colquhoun.

Gill has trained the British Junior and Young Rider teams for over 20 years, during which time they have gained numerous medals. Before turning to training, she won Burghley three-day event, which opened up opportunities within eventing. However, it was making a BBC TV programme on training with David Vine that exposed Gill as a trainer outside the area of her own clientèle. Colonel Allfrey saw these programmes and, on the strength of this, invited her to take on the role of trainer of the Junior three-day event team. This was the start of a great challenge and led on to also training the Young Rider team. Gill is based at The Gill Watson Centre, near Great Missenden, UK, where she gives working pupils and team members an invaluable start as event riders.

More... www.britisheventing.com (accredited trainers list)

TRAINING PHILOSOPHY

■ My main aim when training is to establish a rapport with, and understanding of, both horse and rider. I then work to gain their confidence and progress their level of competence. I try to keep things simple and clear.

■ Jumping exercises can be used to help riders at all levels to achieve balance, rhythm and technique. To try to improve a particular problem, I sometimes find myself inventing an exercise as I go along, because often an exercise that is suitable for one horse is not so good for another and it is important not to press on regardless as that may have a detrimental effect. Using exercises allows the horse to think for himself and aids the rider to sit quietly and not interfere. Working over raised poles can be very beneficial to help establish a good canter, which is vital for jumping.

ADVICE TO NEWCOMERS

Seek good advice and training, to prepare for the tasks ahead; don't run before you can walk.

Introduction to the exercises

Main points to remember

■ Exercises must be chosen to suit the level of the horse, the level of the rider and the attitude of the horse towards the exercise.

■ They are a means of guiding the horse/rider into correct technique, speed and balance.

■ *The eye of the trainer is very important* if the exercise is to be beneficial.

■ Safety is important. Distances need particular care and attention to keep them safe.

Riding reminders

■ Ride through the turns and keep the canter strong enough.

■ Ride into the outside rein and use the corners.

■ Keep your shoulders parallel with the horse's shoulders.

■ Never fight with the horse's mouth. You can keep a contact if you back it up with your leg. You make the rhythm.

Canter exercise to improve its quality and rhythm

Establishing a good canter is essential for jumping; working over raised poles can improve the quality and rhythm of the canter. The raised poles help make the canter more active as the horse has to step higher. By using them on a circle, the horse is encouraged to engage his hind legs further underneath him; this lightens the front end and moves the centre of balance further back. The further back the centre of balance, the easier it is for the horse to raise his forehand. As the poles are the same distance from each other, they automatically help in establishing a rhythm. This is vital, as loss of rhythm leads to loss of balance.

Your horse must be used to walking, trotting and cantering over a single pole, then three poles, on a straight line, before you do this exercise.

SETTING UP

■ Position three poles on the ground on a 25–30m (82–98½ft) circle, off the track at A.

■ Always use heavy poles for ground poles – if possible use blocks of wood to prevent them rolling.

■ Start with the poles slightly further apart than you think you need (see diagram A) and then shorten the distance. It is much easier for the horse to stretch to a longer stride than to collect to a shorter one.

■ The eventual height of the poles and their distance apart depends on your horse's stage of training. Refer to the photos on pp.126-7.

GETTING STARTED

1 Include some shortening and lengthening in canter in your warm-up.

2 Start the exercise with poles on the ground and do not raise them until you are able to ride exactly through the middle of each one.

3 Raise the poles at one end (as shown by the blue poles, diagram A).

4 Be aware that this is a very strenuous exercise for your horse – try running over raised poles yourself and you will see!

PROGRESSING

5 Add three poles on the opposite side of the circle, raised at one end. Then raise all the poles at both ends (Progression 1).

6 Once you can keep the same canter, all the way around the circle, add a pole halfway up each long side (Progression 2). Ride from the circle, over each of these poles and return to the circle. The canter must stay the same throughout.

7 Next, replace the pole with a small upright. A small fence is one you and your horse find easy, and not more than 90cm (3ft). Again, the canter must not alter due to the fence.

How to ride it

■ **Make sure you ride over the centre of each pole.**

■ **Allow the horse to see** what he is doing at least three strides before the poles. As you go over the poles, allow him to see them and to use his back. Give the hand forwards. Keep the weight down through the leg into the heel. Sit still.

■ **The circle should not go all the way to the edge of the arena.** This is so that you will be straight for the fence as you leave the circle (see diagram B).

■ **Return to the circle of raised poles at any time,** to re-establish rhythm.

Fixing common faults

Loss of rhythm: Re-establish the canter on the circle of raised poles and use a pole instead of a fence on the long side.

Anticipation: If the horse speeds up towards the fence on the long side, move it down the arena towards the circle. Reducing the number of strides between the circle and the fence gives the horse less time to increase his pace. If he still speeds up at all, stay on the circle. Use half-halts before the point where he accelerates, as a preventative measure.

Horse is lazy: Make sure you are not asking too much. Is he fit enough?

Tripping over the poles: Make sure you allow your horse to see what he is doing in plenty of time.

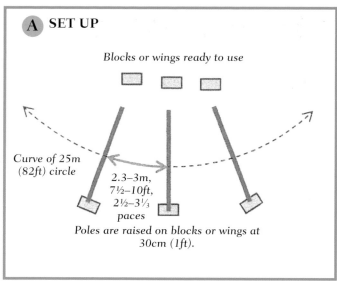

A SET UP

Blocks or wings ready to use

Curve of 25m
(82ft) circle

2.3–3m,
7½–10ft,
2½–3⅓
paces

Poles are raised on blocks or wings at
30cm (1ft).

Distances between poles

- Place the poles 2.3–3m (7½–10ft, 2½–3⅓ paces) apart.
- Use your eye to check the distance while the poles are on the ground.
- Start with a longer distance if you are in any doubt: 2.3m (7½ft) is the *minimum*; most horses will need nearer 3m (10ft).

Arena size

These exercises are intended for use in a 50 x 30m (164 x 98½ft) arena. Bear in mind that using a smaller area increases the difficulty.

*Begin with the poles on the ground, off the track at A.
Then raise them at one end. Progress as shown.*

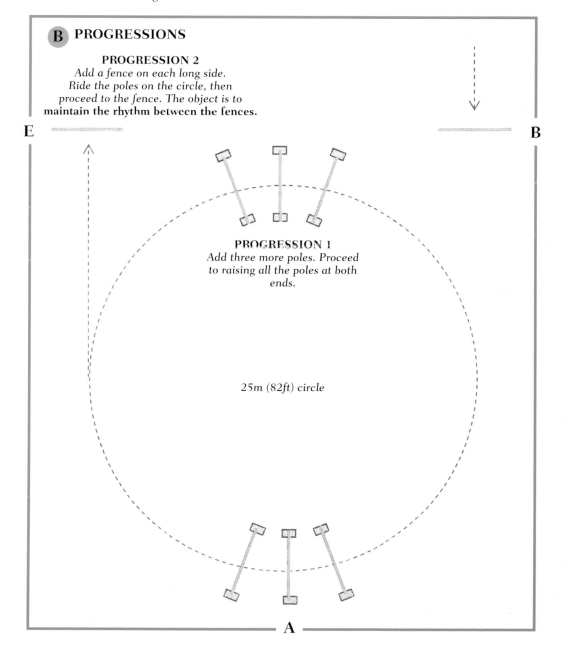

B PROGRESSIONS

PROGRESSION 2
*Add a fence on each long side.
Ride the poles on the circle, then
proceed to the fence. The object is to
maintain the rhythm between the fences.*

E   B

PROGRESSION 1
*Add three more poles. Proceed
to raising all the poles at both
ends.*

25m (82ft) circle

A

PROGRESSING FURTHER

8 The next step is to add some fences at related distances. A related distance helps to test whether or not you are succeeding in keeping the stride length and rhythm constant. Horses get to grips with related distances quite quickly. In the same way that the raised poles assist you to improve the canter, so the related distance will help produce an even stride length.

9 Watch the top show jumpers to see good examples of maintaining rhythm even over very big fences.

Advanced horse
This shows the horse landing and being in very nice balance.

The poles are really too low here. With a more advanced horse, it is quite practical to put the poles up to test its agility even more. Here the horse is looking ahead and his hind legs are jumping through together. The balance of the rider, soft arm and lower leg just make a good balanced picture.

Young horse
This is a young horse, so the poles are set slightly further apart than for the advanced horse. This rider has a good position and a sympathetic feel. I like the balance of the rider, the lower leg position, the softness in the arm, and in the last picture (left), the shoulders just following the movement very slightly. The fact that the rider happens to be looking left is due to a distraction and is not ideal but this rider is so balanced it is not going to make any difference.

C PROGRESSION 3

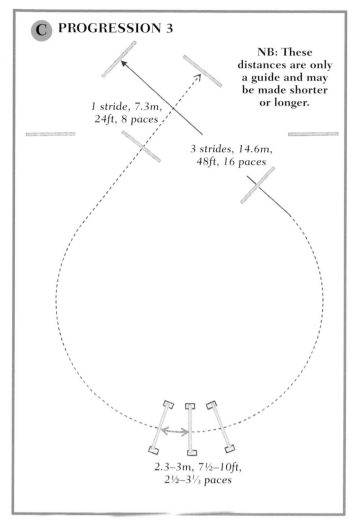

NB: These distances are only a guide and may be made shorter or longer.

1 stride, 7.3m, 24ft, 8 paces

3 strides, 14.6m, 48ft, 16 paces

2.3–3m, 7½–10ft, 2½–3⅓ paces

Add fences at related distances across the arena, removing the raised poles, as required, to use for the central fences.

Right: **A good canter for an advanced horse.** *The hind legs are well engaged, the horse is coming up through the withers and he is focusing on going forwards.*

Right: **A good canter for a young horse.** *The younger horse finds it more difficult to engage the hind leg and although he is going in the right direction, he needs to come up a little more through the withers and have the hind leg a little more underneath him. He could be more upright. In comparison to the more advanced horse, the hind legs are much further out behind him and he is lower in the withers and the poll.*

Fixing common faults

Loss of rhythm: Notice *where* you are losing the rhythm. Likely places are: as you turn for the fences, between the fences and immediately after them. Keep the leg on and ride forwards, maintaining the rhythm.

Loss of rhythm between the fences: Is the distance right for your horse? Does it feel stilted (too short) or like he is stretching (too long)? Make the fences smaller so you can remain in balance at all times.

Loss of rhythm on the turns: Make sure you use your outside aids (outside leg and hand) to balance the horse on the turn, while keeping him coming forwards with both your legs.

More about distances

- Note that distances depend on size of arena, type of surface, position and height of fences, pace of approach (trot or canter) and degree of bend in doglegs (fences at an angle to one another). This is why it is important to be adaptable to the type of horse, rider and situation.
- A normal horse stride is 3.7m (12ft, 4 paces); ponies, depending on size, have 2.7–3.3m (9–11ft, 3–3½ paces) strides.

Trot to canter exercise with variations

Gill Watson

This exercise develops the quality and rhythm of the canter and improves the horse's balance by engaging his hind legs. It is a natural progression of the previous exercise.

SETTING UP

■ Position two fences one on either side of the arena with three trot poles into the first one. Place all the fences off the track.

■ You can divide the arena with poles on the ground and have two horses working at the same time. Change ends to change the rein.

■ The exercise is set so that the landing side of the second fence is going away from the other horse. This is because any loss of control is likely to be more exaggerated by the time the horse has jumped two fences.

GETTING STARTED

1 Trot over the poles to a small upright. Land in canter, on the correct lead, and take any number of strides to the second fence.

2 Return to trot after jumping the second fence. The trot should be the same as it was on the approach to the poles; the rhythm and pace (speed) must not alter.

PROGRESSING

3 Count the number of strides between the first and second fences and aim for a constant number to help establish rhythm.

4 Build up the second fence – make a spread and introduce a filler. This will test whether the quality of the canter is good enough: for example, the canter may be rhythmic but lacking in energy. That could cause the horse to knock a rail down or stop at the spread.

5 Shortening the distance between the trot poles will encourage the hind legs to be more active, which will help to improve the canter.

How to ride it

■ **Look for the second fence** as you are going over the first. This will help you land with the correct lead.

■ **Approach the poles in a good, active working trot.**

Fixing common faults

Landing on the wrong lead: Make sure the horse is 'thinking' in the direction he is going, on the way into and through the poles. He must not be allowed to lean on your inside leg.

Speeding up: If this happens in front of the spread, it means the canter lacked impulsion (energy) to start with. The canter should not change just because the fence has got bigger.

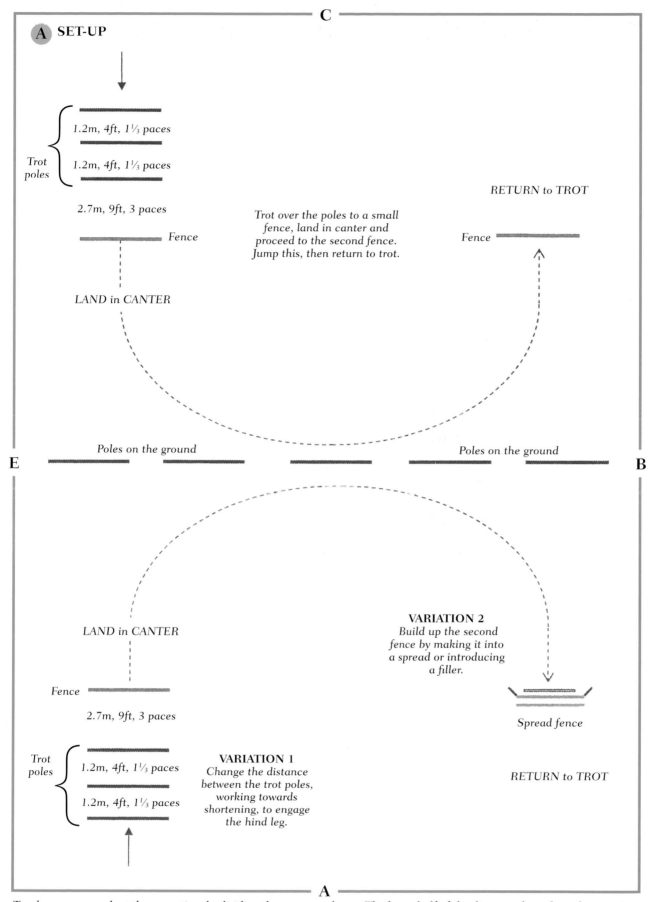

A SET-UP

C

↓

Trot poles {
1.2m, 4ft, 1⅓ paces

1.2m, 4ft, 1⅓ paces
}

2.7m, 9ft, 3 paces

——— Fence

Trot over the poles to a small fence, land in canter and proceed to the second fence. Jump this, then return to trot.

LAND in CANTER

RETURN to TROT

Fence ———

E — Poles on the ground — — Poles on the ground — B

LAND in CANTER

VARIATION 2
Build up the second fence by making it into a spread or introducing a filler.

Fence ———

2.7m, 9ft, 3 paces

Spread fence

Trot poles {
VARIATION 1
Change the distance between the trot poles, working towards shortening, to engage the hind leg.

1.2m, 4ft, 1⅓ paces

1.2m, 4ft, 1⅓ paces
}

RETURN to TROT

↑

A

Two horses can work at the same time by dividing the arena as shown. The lower half of the diagram shows how the exercise can be varied.

Gill Watson

Trot to canter exercise varying from straight to right or left

Uses
- Course preparation
- Rider's focus
- Canter rhythm

Unsuitable for
- This exercise will suit most horses

This exercise is good preparation for riding a course and is the next step on from the previous exercises in this section. Concentration is required to keep the canter through all the related distances.

SETTING UP

- Place a single pole on the ground where the cross pole and each of the three other fences will be built (diagram A). The placing pole is not needed until the cross pole is built.
- Put a pole on the ground in the two corners before the cross pole to encourage a good turn and a straight approach to it, from either rein.

GETTING STARTED

1 Start the exercise over poles on the ground to establish balance, rhythm and control.

2 Approach from the horse's best rein to begin with. The direct route is the easiest, so ride that a few times before riding the left- or right-hand routes.

3 To vary the exercise, change the distances either to alter the number of strides required or to ask for a longer or shorter stride

PROGRESSING

4 Next, set up a cross pole with a placing pole in front of it (diagram A). Ride the cross to each of the poles on the ground first, then build up the rest of the fences as shown. Making the fence on the central route into a spread encourages the horse to enjoy the exercise and keeps him fresh between tackling the trickier right and left routes.

5 Move on to the progression in diagram B once exercise A is going well. Build five fences, jumpable either way, and jump each individually.

6 Start to link fences, in order to ride different related distances. Notice which way your horse finds easier. Perhaps you favour one side too?

7 Link all the fences together to make a course.

How to ride it
- **It is essential to make a straight approach** to the placing pole. To this end, use ground poles in the corners, as indicated.
- **Make your intended route clear to your horse.** Ensure you are looking where you mean to go, while going over the cross pole.
- **All points mentioned for the previous exercise** also apply to this one.

Fixing common faults
Poor turn after the fence: Start looking and planning earlier.

Distances
These distances are only a guide, based on a 3.7m (12ft) stride length. They can be varied to change the number of strides or to get the horse to shorten or lengthen.

A SET-UP

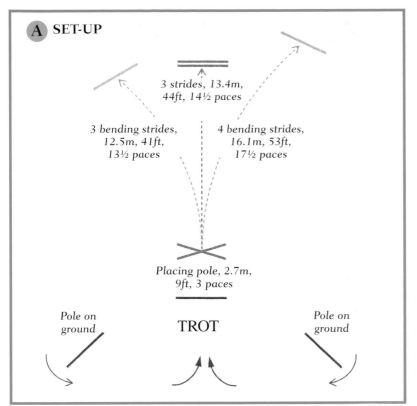

3 strides, 13.4m, 44ft, 14½ paces

3 bending strides, 12.5m, 41ft, 13½ paces

4 bending strides, 16.1m, 53ft, 17½ paces

Placing pole, 2.7m, 9ft, 3 paces

Pole on ground

Pole on ground

TROT

Place a single pole where each fence will be built. The placing pole is not needed until the cross pole is built.

B PROGRESSION

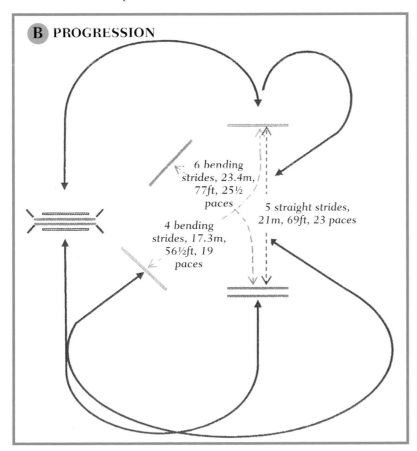

6 bending strides, 23.4m, 77ft, 25½ paces

5 straight strides, 21m, 69ft, 23 paces

4 bending strides, 17.3m, 56½ft, 19 paces

Build five fences that can be jumped from both directions. Start by jumping them individually and then begin to link them to ride different related distances.

Right: **Bending strides:** *The rider is focusing on riding the bend and then getting straight so that the hind legs are directly behind the front legs before take-off. The horse is very neat in front, as he takes off over the centre of the fence. Both horse and rider appear in good balance.*

Distances

These distances are guidelines for training purposes. It is better to make them too long than too short and they are for normal length strides rather than shortened or lengthened ones.

It is important to train your eye as distance charts are no substitute for being able to see what is actually happening. Remember that as the fences are raised, the distances will need to be adjusted accordingly.

Distances in training depend on:

- The size of the fences.
- The horse's length of stride.
- The education of the horse.
- The rider's ability to establish a good canter.

ALL DISTANCES ARE FOR HORSES 15.2hh and over		PACES	FEET	METRES
BETWEEN POLES				
Approached in trot				
Trotting poles	min	$1\frac{1}{3}$	4	1.2
	max	$1\frac{2}{3}$–2	5'6	1.7
Place pole in front of fence	min	3	9	2.7
	max	$3\frac{1}{3}$	10	3
Place pole after fence	min	$3\frac{1}{3}$	10	3
Approached in Canter				
Canter poles	min	3	9	2.7
	max	$3\frac{2}{3}$	11	3.4
Place pole in front of fence	min	$3\frac{1}{3}$	10	3
	max	$3\frac{2}{3}$	11	3.4
Place pole after fence (1)	min	$3\frac{1}{3}$	10	3
	max	$3\frac{2}{3}$	11	3.4
BETWEEN FENCES				
Approached in canter (2)				
One stride	min	7	21	6.4
	max	8 - $8\frac{1}{3}$	24.5	7.5
Two strides	min	11	33	10
	max	12	36	11
Three strides	min	15	45	13.7
	max	16	48	14.6
Four strides	min	19	57	17.4
	max	20	60	18.3
Five strides	min	22	66	20.1
Between bounce fences				
Bounce	min	$3\frac{1}{3}$	10	3
	max	4	12	3.7

(1) Do not place a pole after a fence for a very novice horse or rider.

(2) If you approach in trot the distance between the first and second fence may need to be shortened by up to 3ft.

Glossary

Ahead of the movement

A rider is ahead of the movement or 'in front of his horse' when his own centre of balance is ahead of the horse's. It frequently happens in front of fences, with the rider leaning forwards before the horse has taken off. This is the worst and most dangerous fault for a cross-country rider and it is the most common cause of falls or refusals. Note that a rider can be in the forward seat without being in front of the movement.

Behind the leg

The horse should move forwards as soon as the leg is applied. If he is behind the leg, then as soon as the leg is taken off, the horse slows or even stops. When the leg is applied, he does not respond immediately.

This is the next most serious fault after being ahead of the movement. This is the opposite to being in front of the leg – see below.

Forward seat

The rider remains in jumping position so that his seat is only very lightly brushing the saddle. Refer to George Morris' section for more information.

Going out through the shoulder

The horse bends his neck too much to one side (the inside) which opens out the shoulder joint on the outside (of the bend). From this position he is able to move through that outside shoulder, away from the direction he is bent. The only way to regain control is to straighten the neck. To do that you must use the outside rein and outside leg. As the horse will be leaning on that leg, you must take it away from his side completely and then use it sharply, on the girth rather than behind it, to help close the shoulder. Aim to bend the horse slightly in the opposite direction and keep him there, whichever way you are going, until he remains straight when you release him.

Ground line

The part of a fence which touches the ground on the take-off side. The horse uses the ground line to judge his take-off point. Create a ground line by placing a ground pole at the base of the fence or slightly in front of it. The further in front the pole lies, the more inviting for the horse. However, much more than 1ft away and you risk confusing the horse into thinking he should canter over the pole first. To jump a fence from either direction, use two ground poles, one on each side of the fence. A *false* ground line is one that is underneath the fence and hence fools the horse into taking off too late. A shadow can also create a ground line, true or false depending on where it falls. For schooling the ground line should always be at or in front of the front of the fence.

Ground pole

A pole on the ground, preferably a heavy pole so that it does not move easily or break if trodden on. Ground poles in the diagrams in this book are black, for easy identification.

Half-halt

This is a subtle set of aids to increase the energy and move the centre of balance further back. They can be used at any time and in any pace except over a pole or jump. The idea is to rebalance the horse, making it easier for him to stop, go, or turn. To make a half-halt, sit up, and, at the same moment as squeezing both reins, use both legs to make the horse 'jump up' underneath you. This will cause his hind legs to engage further underneath him. Too little rein, and he will simply speed up. Too much rein, and he will stop. Too much leg into an immobile hand and he may rear or plunge. Half-halts are useful for preventative purposes, for example before going downhill, to stop the horse's balance going on to his forehand. The strength of the aids used varies from an almost imperceptible thought to your whole body strength. At their minimum they are used for communication, as a 'hello' to warn the horse some other instructions are on the way. Used consistently, half-halts are the means by which you explain what is coming up next; for example, to tell the horse that what appears to be a spread fence is actually a bounce.

In front of the leg

The horse should always be in front of the leg. When the leg is applied, the horse must respond immediately. The rider must not have to work just to maintain forward movement.

On the forehand

The horse is on his forehand if his centre of gravity is too far forwards. The horse is likely to try to lean on the rider's hands and the rider will have the feeling of the horse 'going downhill'. Because the horse's balance is too far forwards, he will find it impossible to stop or turn quickly – as you would if running down hill, leaning forwards. Most young horses are on the forehand as it takes considerable training to move the balance back.

Opening the rein

The inside hand (inside the bend) moves sideways to guide the horse. The hand does not pull back during this movement. Refer to Jane Holderness-Roddam's section for more information.

Propping

This occurs when the horse puts in a short half stride in an abrupt manner before take-off. It gives the rider an unpleasant jarring feeling. It happens when the horse has got too close to a fence, usually a vertical. It is corrected by encouraging the horse to take off further away from the fence.

Rider Profiles

Helen Cole

Helen has ridden at Advanced and 3-star level. As well as working part-time for the Countryside Agency in Bristol, she has also been developing a livery and training yard at Stockley Farm, Wiltshire, over the last two years. As a BHSII, she also teaches a number of private clients and various Pony Clubs. However, her main focus is on producing some young horses that she hopes will go on to Advanced level.

Daisy Dick

Daisy show jumped at Young Rider level before she turned to eventing; a change that resulted in team bronze in 1992 and team gold in 1993 at the Young Rider European Championships. As a senior, she has achieved several placings at Badminton, beginning in 1997 when she was 7th on Headley Bravo. Then in 2004 and 2005 she was 11th and 8th with her best-ever horse, Spring Along. Blenheim Europeans followed where the combination finished 11th. They are currently listed for the World Equestrian Games in Aachen 2006.

Antoinette McKeowen

Antoinette has ridden at Advanced level for several years. In 2005, she was long-listed for the Athens Olympics and short-listed for the Blenheim European Championships. She has completed Badminton four times and in 2003 was placed 12th. She also achieved 12th place at Blenheim in 2001. Antoinette is based in Penton, near Andover where she has four advanced horses plus several up-and-coming youngsters.

Marcus Reid

Marcus has ridden at Advanced level in eventing and Prix St George level in dressage. He rides several stallions for the Catherston and Biddesden Studs and has achieved success in both dressage and eventing. In 2000 he won the Novice Eventing Championships, then in 2001, he won two National Championships in medium level dressage. He is currently producing a new team of young horses that he hopes to take to the Olympics one day.

Darrell Scaife

Darrell has had several 3-day event wins and has achieved a 12th place at Burghley. He spent 11 years with Jane Holderness-Roddam, learning his trade in preparation for setting up on his own. He is currently based at Jayne Nicholson's yard in Devizes where he has eight horses including Burghley Young Event horse winner Zeus of Rushall. Darrell is a BE accredited trainer and a listed dressage judge.

A special thanks to the extra riders in Pat Burgess's section: Amanda Barton p.18, Jane Brewer p.18, Laura Creese p.18, Kate Elstob p.21, Kate Robb p.25 (top), and Marion Watts p.27.

Caroline Orme

Caroline trained as a working pupil at the Catherston Stud with Jennie Loriston-Clarke, at Aston Park with Gill Watson and at the Wirral. As a BHSII she is a part-time freelance instructor. Caroline lives near Andover in Hampshire, UK.

Acknowledgments

Sue and Rod Bennett and Jayne Nicholson for the use of their arenas. Pat Burgess for giving lots of time when she didn't have any via several 11pm meetings at what became 'our' service station! Tina Butler, for some great photos in George Morris' section. Peter Fitzsimons. Lucinda Green for significantly improving my technical knowledge through her clinics. Clive Hamblin for lending some jumps. Jane Holderness-Roddam without whose advice and support this book would not have been possible. Jennie Loriston-Clarke. Sharon Paul for the use of her horse, 'Radish', for the lunging exercise. Jo Stevens who was indispensable and helped with all aspects of the book. Gill Watson for inspiring the idea and helping to get it off the ground. And all the contributors, all of whom put so much into their sections. Kit Houghton for taking wonderful photos and all the riders for doing a fantastic job, on immaculately turned out horses – and especially for putting up with some of my more mad-cap ideas! Finally, all at Blue Bell Farm, Penton, for 'ask the audience' duties.

Additional thanks to British Eventing and USEF for biography statistics and website references. Kate Green for a press pass and use of material from *Training the Young Horse* (Pippa Funnell) and *Schooling for Success* (William Fox-Pitt). *The Masters of Eventing* by G. W. Freeman, for inspiring the format.

For further information on Virginia Elliot's training methods, see *Training the Event Horse*, written by Ginny with Genevieve Murphy and originally published by Stanley Paul. It has proved to be a useful source in the preparation of Ginny's chapter.

Picture Acknowledgments

All the photographs in this book were provided by Kit Houghton, except the following:
Pat Burgess, page 18 (all black and white photographs); Tina Butler, pages 102, 104, 105 and 108; Chronicle of the Horse/Tricia Booker, page 103; Expo Life, page 110; Sheila Fitzsimons, page 51 (right); Jane Holderness-Roddam, pages 72 (photograph by Clive Hiles) and 73; © Trevor Meeks/Horse & Hound/IPC+ Syndication, pages 33 and 55; Caroline Orme, pages 18 (all colour photographs), 21 (bottom), 25 (top, centre left and centre right), 27, and 51 (left); Fiona Scott-Maxwell, pages 65 and 83; © Stephen Sparkes/Helen Revington, page 32; and Gill Watson, pages 122 and 123.